Hilary Kingsley has been writing about television in newspapers and magazines since 1975. In 1990, she was named National Broadcast Journalist of the Year. She is the author of *Soap Box*, described by *The Sunday Times* as 'the most entertaining dictionary since Dr Johnson's', and co-author with Geoff Tibballs of *Box of Delights*, *The Golden Years of Television*.

A devoted *EastEnders*' fan, Hilary looks forward to the day when Dot Cotton becomes Prime Minister or, at least, Director General of the BBC.

Ethel in defence of Dot:

'She was two penn'orth of God 'elp us. She grew up, she got 'er 'eart's desire and she got married. She got married to a pig. He got her pregnant and then made her get rid of it. And then there was Nick. 'E tried to kill 'er.'

That's why I love *EastEnders*.   HILARY KINGSLEY

EastEnders
HANDBOOK

HILARY KINGSLEY

BBC BOOKS

Published by BBC Books,
a division of BBC Enterprises Limited,
Woodlands, 80 Wood Lane, London W12 0TT

First published 1991

ISBN 0–563–36292–8

Editor Jane Struthers

Designed by Roger Daniels

Set in Galliard by Ace Filmsetting Limited, Frome
Printed and bound in Great Britain by Clays Ltd, St Ives Plc
Colour separations by Dot Gradations, Chelmsford
Cover printed by Clays Ltd, St Ives Plc

CONTENTS

Being the Boss

Michael Ferguson.

*E*astEnders is an extraordinary programme. Unpredictable. And a bit dangerous. Sometimes a bit daft, sometimes a bit upsetting. Often very moving. Everybody seems to have an opinion about it: 'It's depressing'; 'It's boring'; 'Bring back Den and Angie.' Even people who claim they never watch it still have strong views. Curiously, everyone who doesn't watch it knows someone who does. Liking it or not, about a third of the British population watch every episode.

What is it that makes this never-ending story about a handful of imaginary people so compelling? Diane Butcher runs away from home and there are sightings of her all over the British Isles. Nick Cotton claims he has found religion and raises a storm of indignation. Mark Fowler admits he's HIV positive and the waiting rooms of special clinics up and down the country are suddenly packed.

Why do we care what happens to these ordinary people? Well, it certainly isn't the glamour: any viewer searching for escapism shouldn't head for Walford. And it's hardly because of the thrilling action: in some episodes Pauline washing the dishes or Dot mixing up the service washes in the launderette causes the most excitement. Snappy, sophisticated dialogue? Lots of laughs? Not usually.

What it's all about, of course, is you and me and everyone. It's about the problems of living, of belonging to families, of illness and disappointment, frustration and facing up to fear, anger, jealousy, death. It's about occasional success and happiness and going a bit mad every now and again and all the other too-elusive joys of life.

Drama is sometimes described as life with the boring bits taken out. The challenge is to create the interesting bits that are left in.

I joined the team that meets that challenge in the autumn of 1989. I'd started my career as an actor, moved into directing on such programmes as *Compact*, *The Newcomers*, *The Doctors* and action series such as *The Sandbaggers* and *Airline*. Most recently I'd been a producer on *The Bill*.

This was different. In the first months my task was to get to know *EastEnders*. I'd watched it, of course, and admired it. But my family, especially my daughters Nikki and Tracy, who are in their twenties, often had to fill me in on the details of stories. Suddenly, I had to know everything. I wished I'd had this book then as a guide, I can tell you. I took home all the 'back stories' from our script department and one weekend I just read and read and read.

I was keen to talk to the actors individually because they're the people who know the characters best. I found no prima donnas but serious, committed people who wanted to give the very best performances they could. I wanted to build on their strengths.

Diane's time as a runaway was my first experience of a hard, controversial story, and the programme was number one in the ratings.

Later, Mo's suffering from Alzheimer's Disease gave people permission to talk about an illness that had been almost too distressing to discuss in public before. Viewers told us we'd given them a shorthand – 'like Mo', 'like Disa' when that character was revealed as a victim of sexual abuse and, of course, 'like Mark'.

Nearly two years later I still find it a strange and worrying business, manipulating the lives of these imaginary people who have become friends to millions. Every week the producers and editors meet to thrash out a pathway into the future. Sometimes one story takes over like a spirited animal that knows where it's going and doesn't want anyone on its back. Another will dig in its hooves and refuse to move. There are arguments and compromises and every now and then blessed harmony.

The stories emerge at last, the writers turn ideas into scenes, the directors and performers turn the scenes into life. Eventually it's there on-screen to be commented on, gossiped about, shouted at or cheered.

I've got used to the criticism, both good and bad. But every Friday when the viewing figures start printing out and we're still up there, jostling with our rivals for the top spot, it's rewarding to know that, for another week at least, plenty of you are still coming round to the Square.

How long will *EastEnders* last? I really don't know but I bet it'll be a few years before the bulldozers start knocking down Albert Square. One day, perhaps, there'll be a preservation order on it. It certainly deserves to be looked after.

MICHAEL FERGUSON
Executive Producer
September 1989–July 1991

How it all began

Julia Smith with Keith Harris on the set.

EastEnders changed British soap opera. Indeed, it changed British television drama altogether. It's even fair to say that, in some small ways, the programme changed the British way of life.

The show was born at 7 p.m. on 19 February 1985, when the first episode was screened. Seventeen million people were present at the birth – the size of the first night audience. (It has often risen above 20 million since.) But, of course, the BBC's first proper soap opera ('drama serial', if you prefer the grander terminology of broadcasting brass) had a long, long gestation period.

Exactly when the conception occurred is hard to say. You could choose 14 March 1983 when Julia Smith and Tony Holland, respectively producer and script writer of *District Nurse*, were first asked by the BBC if they would take on a bi-weekly soap. They said they would, but it was not until 2 February 1984 that their one-page 300-word format, hurriedly cobbled together over a drink in a wine bar, was accepted by the Controller of BBC 1. Or you could argue that the success of one of Julia's earlier efforts, *Angels*, a bi-weekly (but not year-round) series about hospital nurses, that began in 1976, was what made the BBC try for true soap operas seven years later. You could add that in the early 1980s, when the BBC seemed to have lost the ratings battle and there was pressure for change from Westminster, the idea was to invade ITV's territory, popular drama, in a new and aggressive way.

It wasn't an easy pregnancy at all. The new baby would not be a poppet but instead a screaming, kicking child of the times. The next problem was where should it live? Real East End locations were considered – Fassett Square in Hackney was well in the running – but the problems of non-stop shooting in a working London location were immense.

The BBC had bought Elstree Studios in January 1984 and, after a lot of to-ing and fro-ing, if-ing and but-ing, it was decided to build Albert Square as a permanent outdoor set on a piece of wasteland there.

To ensure it all looked right, plenty of East End squares were investigated and photographed. Keith Harris and his team of clever designers found a way to make the Elstree set look more like a crumbling bit of Victorian

East London than the real thing, much of which had been gentrified.

They succeeded. Their wood and fibreglass fake has proved so sturdy that the fierce gales of 1987 and later haven't brought down so much as a chimney stack, let alone a garden gate. But what was the new baby going to be called? For months it was *East 8*, although *London Pride* was also on the cards for a time, until *EastEnders* got the thumbs-up. Julia Smith finally hit on the title when she realised she had been using it for months in discussions about the programme.

There was still a long way to go. There were huge logistical headaches to sort out, difficulties with unions and, once the major characters had been set down in writing, problems finding suitable actors, actors with stamina, prepared to look and sound rough and ready. Then came the search for writers who knew about London with the lid off.

Julia Smith, series producer, and Tony Holland, script editor, never stopped working during this run-up period. They'd gone off to Lanzarote so they could work in peace while creating the characters – Den and Angie, Pauline and Arthur, Sue and Ali – but that was only the start of their labours. The pair had co-operated off and on since 1971 when they worked on *Z Cars* together. Later on, *Angels*

PLASTIC DAFFS AND 800 WEEDS

Building Albert Square, not in Victorian times but in a matter of months in 1984, with the specification that it should last about fifteen years, took great skill, On the set, brilliantly designed by Keith Harris at a cost of about £750,000, the houses which look so solid are made from plastic bricks over steel skeletons. The overhead 'iron' railway bridge is painted plywood with varnished damp patches. A train was seen crossing it only once, on the day of Lou's funeral. It didn't strain the structure because it was a ten-second illusion, cleverly produced in the BBC's electronic workshop. It cost 'an arm and a leg' but old Lou was worth it.

At the start of the series, around 800 weeds were planted in the gardens. Plastic daffodils had to be stuck into the ground in February to look right when the episodes were screened in April. And on Arthur's allotment the lettuces are usually fine specimens from a Hertfordshire hydro-culture centre, produced long before they might grow outdoors and swiftly planted as the cameras arrive.

Back in 1984, workmen were appalled when they were ordered to chip brand-new kerb stones and patch up a perfect, newly laid tarmac road. White net curtains had to be sprayed with hair lacquer to make them look suitably old and grubby. Monica Boggust, the scenic props buyer, and her team had to trawl around junk shops and auctions searching for the sorts of ornaments and pictures that Lou would have liked. The heavy fringed cloth they found for her living room is so difficult to replace that it has had to be patched and stitched during the programme's life.

9

and *District Nurse* brought them together again. They shared a friendship and a philosophy that popular drama could deal with important issues and, with the help of three-dimensional characters, interwoven storylines and fast, short scenes, entertain and hold a mass audience.

Granada's *Coronation Street* has successfully used a single street to define its world for a quarter of a century. It worked well, sometimes brilliantly, but the Northern soap never suggested a true sense of community at that time. The characters, colourful though they were, just happened to live near each other. The same was true of *Brookside*, Channel 4's socially and politically aware soap, which was born in 1982.

EastEnders was going to be different. There would be two main families, the Beales and the Fowlers, but in a way the whole of Albert Square was to be seen as one big family, held together by the bonds of time, need, friendship, even by feuds and enmity. There would be no rich people, no one who was smug or safe. Albert Square was a microcosm of East London, and perhaps of the whole of working-class London.

It was a big concept and it worked from the start. Typically, soap operas start off slow and build. *EastEnders* started fast with a big audience. That fell away slightly when Yorkshire Television's *Emmerdale Farm* was screened at the same time, but when the Tuesday and Thursday 7.30 p.m. slot was cleared for *EastEnders*, its audience grew, climbed high and stayed high.

Young people, who would not usually have been caught watching anything that appealed to 'wrinklies', were hooked by the honest talk and gritty themes. It wasn't surprising. Episode One opened with Dennis Watts, Arthur Fowler and Ali Osman kicking in the door of a council flat to find Reg Cox, a cantankerous old codger who hadn't been seen for days, dead in his armchair.

There were two things to notice about that. Firstly, the real social issue – the plight of the elderly poor who live alone – was tackled head on. Many more social issues were to follow. Secondly, four men were involved in this crucial opening incident. Traditionally, soap opera is aimed at women and is largely about women; sometimes the men in soaps are not much more than accessories.

In *EastEnders*, however, there was going to be balance: the sexes were to get equal opportunities. Arthur's unemployment, breakdown and subsequent imprisonment

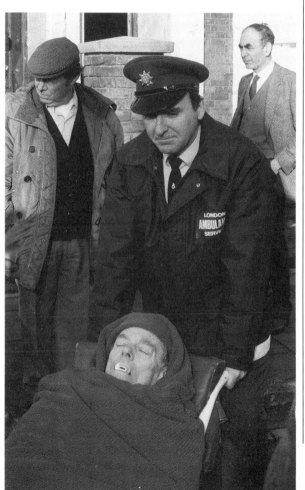

**Left: The first episode. Above: The Fowler family.
Below right: Pete and Den in the pub.**

touched the whole country. Den's clashes with Angie brought *EastEnders* to a peak of popularity and toppled *Coronation Street* from the top of the ratings charts. (There were arguments about the way the audiences were measured. The two great soaps have continued to fight it out, dominating the ratings between them.) Lofty's disappointments brought tears to our eyes; we understood why Colin left the Square and sympathised . . .

There have been few social issues that *EastEnders* hasn't examined. Abortion, cot death, unemployment, promiscuity, sexual abuse, single parenthood, Aids . . . write your own list. So well have these topics been tackled that I believe they have changed the way we ordinary people think about them and judge our own experiences.

In 1988 Julia Smith, affectionately called The Godmother, left her growing baby to

work on other projects. Tony Holland also moved on. Mike Gibbon took over at the helm, followed in the autumn of 1989 by Michael Ferguson, fresh from the acclaimed bi-weekly Thames TV police series *The Bill*. Albert Square was not suddenly swarming with cussing coppers as might have been feared. But the excitement certainly didn't flag and the thought-provoking controversies continued to hook millions, worry Mrs Mary Whitehouse and grab newspaper headlines.

Albert Square's male residents have continued to be given major storylines. We worry about Mark being HIV positive, Grant's brainstorms, Ian Beale's developing ruthlessness. But that doesn't mean the women are unimportant in the series. How could we not care about Pauline's perils, Dot's dilemmas or Kathy's concerns?

EastEnders has forced other soap operas – British ones, anyway, and particularly *Coronation Street* – to abandon some of their cosiness and easy sentimentality and go bravely for life with all its dangers.

Since 19 February 1985, soap opera has changed. These days, it's got to feel real.

Lives, Loves and Links

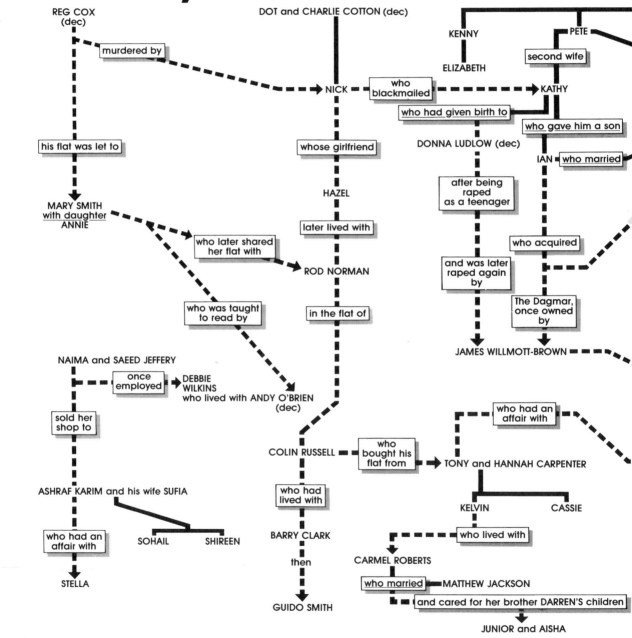

REG COX (dec)

murdered by

DOT and CHARLIE COTTON (dec)

KENNY

ELIZABETH

PETE

second wife

NICK — who blackmailed — KATHY

who had given birth to

who gave him a son

his flat was let to

whose girlfriend

DONNA LUDLOW (dec)

IAN — who married

MARY SMITH with daughter ANNIE

HAZEL

after being raped as a teenager

who later shared her flat with

later lived with

who acquired

ROD NORMAN

and was later raped again by

who was taught to read by

in the flat of

The Dagmar, once owned by

NAIMA and SAEED JEFFERY

once employed → DEBBIE WILKINS who lived with ANDY O'BRIEN (dec)

JAMES WILLMOTT-BROWN

sold her shop to

who had an affair with

COLIN RUSSELL — who bought his flat from → TONY and HANNAH CARPENTER

ASHRAF KARIM and his wife SUFIA

who had lived with

KELVIN

CASSIE

who had an affair with

SOHAIL

SHIREEN

BARRY CLARK

who lived with

then

CARMEL ROBERTS

STELLA

GUIDO SMITH

who married ■ MATTHEW JACKSON

and cared for her brother DARREN'S children

JUNIOR and AISHA

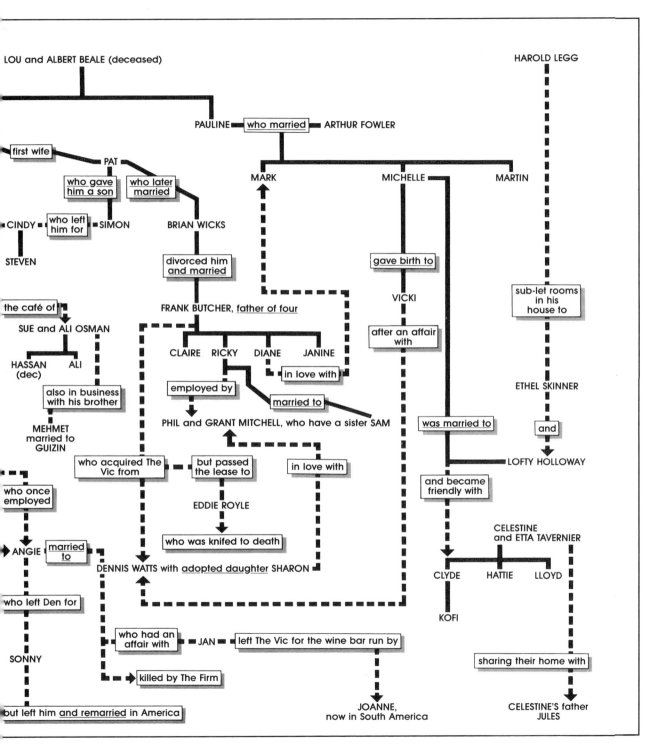

LOU and ALBERT BEALE (deceased)

HAROLD LEGG

PAULINE — who married — ARTHUR FOWLER

first wife

PAT

who gave him a son | who later married

MARK | MICHELLE | MARTIN

CINDY — who left him for — SIMON

BRIAN WICKS

STEVEN

divorced him and married

gave birth to

VICKI

sub-let rooms in his house to

the café of

FRANK BUTCHER, father of four

after an affair with

SUE and ALI OSMAN

HASSAN (dec) | ALI

CLAIRE | RICKY | DIANE | JANINE

in love with

ETHEL SKINNER

also in business with his brother

employed by

married to

was married to

and

MEHMET married to GUIZIN

PHIL and GRANT MITCHELL, who have a sister SAM

who acquired The Vic from | but passed the lease to | in love with

LOFTY HOLLOWAY

who once employed

EDDIE ROYLE

and became friendly with

ANGIE — married to

who was knifed to death

CELESTINE and ETTA TAVERNIER

DENNIS WATTS with adopted daughter SHARON

CLYDE | HATTIE | LLOYD

who left Den for

KOFI

who had an affair with — JAN — left The Vic for the wine bar run by

SONNY

killed by The Firm

sharing their home with

but left him and remarried in America

JOANNE, now in South America

CELESTINE'S father JULES

13

Life in the Square

The inspiration for the set.

You could say the foundations of Albert Square in the London Borough of Walford were laid in the last century: its name comes from Albert, the Prince Consort. His Queen, Victoria, is herself commemorated in the name of the pub where her effigy still surveys the bar.

The terraced houses which form the Square were built then, and the ones that survived the two World Wars are sturdy enough, but have been given a miss by the pebble-dash, stone-cladding and double-glazing salesmen. Some houses, such as Dr Legg's, are privately owned, but some are converted into flats. Some, like Dot's, the Fowlers' and the Taverniers', are rented from the council. Some stand vacant and boarded up, so tramps, squatters and people made homeless and jobless in the harsh 1980s sometimes stay there. Other passers-through include drug users and those who survive by thieving.

Yet the place is small enough for it to feel like a village, and with Dot Cotton's Neighbourhood Watch most residents feel safe and among friends. Children play and people meet in the gardens, which are run down for want of cash and attention, though Fowler and Son have now won a contract to tend them. The sporting man has the betting shop and, although we haven't seen it, there's the local football club, Walford Town, commonly known as 'The Wallies'. And, of course, there's gossip in the launderette, Dot's domain, used by the Fowler family and at one time by Pat Butcher for all the laundry from the B & B. Couldn't she afford a washing machine of her own? Well, yes, but the B & B set in which to put it had not been built!

Social upheavals seem to have missed Albert Square. A few yuppies came to The Dagmar before it went up in flames. Strokes Wine Bar did not survive the hasty departure of the gangsters who owned it. And visitors to the Square – sadly, not big-spending Japanese or American tourists but reps, lorry drivers and the like – stay at the B & B guest house, once owned by the easy-going Doris, now by Pat and Frank Butcher. It may not be Claridges, but at least it's a lot cosier than the Crossroads Motel.

'Viewers notice every detail,' said scenic props boss Monica Boggust. 'Some write and ask if they can buy the items because they like the plates or the pictures; even Pauline's potato peeler. We have to disappoint them. A lady even asked to take Sharon's unwanted wardrobe off her hands. We had to explain that it was due to go back to the furniture store.'

They also have offers for the cars: twenty of them owned by the programme, each taxed and up to date with MOT certificates. Some are on sale in Frank's car lot, while others are used by characters or parked as props. But the most expensive (and flashiest) motor, Frank's Mercedes, is hired. So when Phil drove into it, the dent and scratch it received were fake. There is also a red double-decker London bus parked in the bus station, bought specially for the programme.

Fans don't ask for the metal Albert Square signs, though: they prefer to climb over the walls at Elstree and steal them. For a time the answer was to put up plastic signs which could be removed easily. At least the walls and railings weren't likely to be damaged that way!

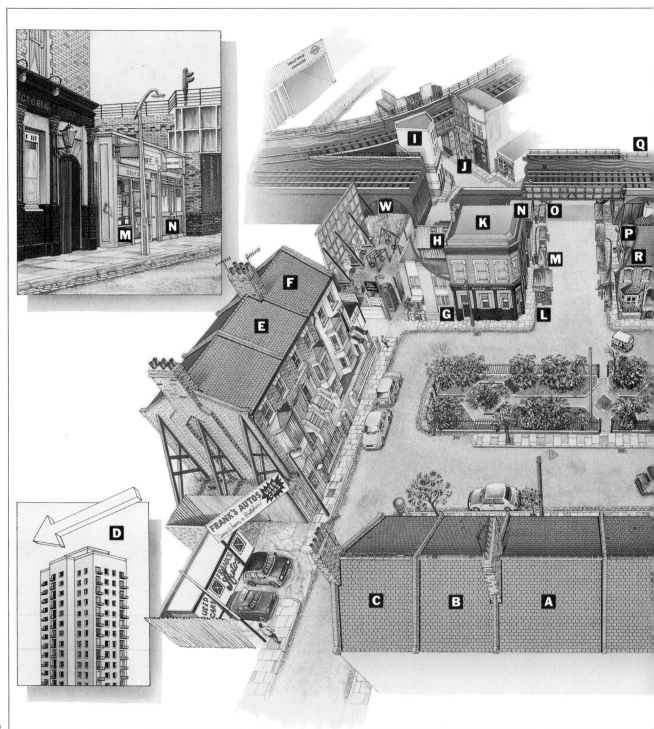

Who Lives Where

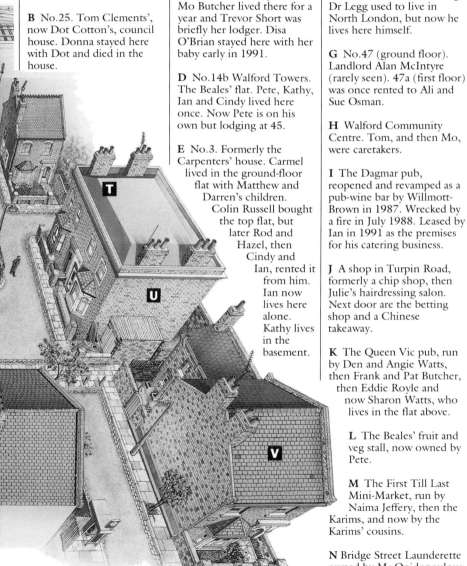

A No.27. The Taverniers – Celestine, Etta, Hattie, Lloyd, Clyde, Kofi and Jules – live here.

B No.25. Tom Clements', now Dot Cotton's, council house. Donna stayed here with Dot and died in the house.

C No.23. Vacant. Sue, Ali and Hassan Osman lived downstairs, Reg Cox, then Mary and Annie, upstairs. Mo Butcher lived there for a year and Trevor Short was briefly her lodger. Disa O'Brian stayed here with her baby early in 1991.

D No.14b Walford Towers. The Beales' flat. Pete, Kathy, Ian and Cindy lived here once. Now Pete is on his own but lodging at 45.

E No.3. Formerly the Carpenters' house. Carmel lived in the ground-floor flat with Matthew and Darren's children. Colin Russell bought the top flat, but later Rod and Hazel, then Cindy and Ian, rented it from him. Ian now lives here alone. Kathy lives in the basement.

F No.1. Dr Legg's surgery and maisonette. Ethel and Lofty had flats here. Ethel moved to sheltered housing. Dr Legg used to live in North London, but now he lives here himself.

G No.47 (ground floor). Landlord Alan McIntyre (rarely seen). 47a (first floor) was once rented to Ali and Sue Osman.

H Walford Community Centre. Tom, and then Mo, were caretakers.

I The Dagmar pub, reopened and revamped as a pub-wine bar by Willmott-Brown in 1987. Wrecked by a fire in July 1988. Leased by Ian in 1991 as the premises for his catering business.

J A shop in Turpin Road, formerly a chip shop, then Julie's hairdressing salon. Next door are the betting shop and a Chinese takeaway.

K The Queen Vic pub, run by Den and Angie Watts, then Frank and Pat Butcher, then Eddie Royle and now Sharon Watts, who lives in the flat above.

L The Beales' fruit and veg stall, now owned by Pete.

M The First Till Last Mini-Market, run by Naima Jeffery, then the Karims, and now by the Karims' cousins.

N Bridge Street Launderette owned by Mr Opidopoulous.

O The stall that was Kathy's wool and woollens stall.

P The Bridge Street Café, formerly Ali's Café run by Sue and Ali Osman, then taken over by Ian Beale, now run by Kathy, Pauline and Frank.

Q Henry's Wine Bar, then Strokes' Wine Bar run by Joanne Francis and Dennis Watts. Now the Pizza Parlour.

R No. 45. Lou Beale's council house. Now the Fowlers – Pauline, Arthur, Mark and Martin – live here.

S No.43. Debbie Wilkins and Andy O'Brien, then James Willmott-Brown, lived in the house. Then it was converted into flats. Sharon, Michelle and Vicki lived in 43a, the flat Dennis Watts bought. Joanne bought 43b, then sold it to Julie Cooper who sold it to Phil Mitchell. Grant Mitchell bought Sharon's flat in 1990.

T No.18. The Butchers' – Frank, Pat, Janine and now Ricky with Sam – live here with Diane when she's home. Connecting door to . . .

U No.20. The B & B owned by Doris, now by Frank and Pat Butcher and where Dot works.

V Victoria Road. The Karim's house, now occupied by Rachel Kominsky. Karen lodged here, followed by Michelle and Vicki.

W Phil and Grant's workshop.

V ictoria had been on the throne half a century when the Albert Square public house was built, in the style of thousands of others, during the 1880s. With its traditional 'gin palace' windows and dark wood furniture it has always been a place for strong drink, strong talk and loud noise.

If the old Queen saw how it has changed over the years she might not be amused, but Walford folk think it's comfortable and jolly, at any rate. When we first got to know it there were separate public and saloon bars, but Den and Angie hired Tony Carpenter to knock down the division between the two.

Since then the decor has changed little. The gaudily painted effigy of Victoria continues to loom across the bar and the walls are still adorned with pictures of the Prince and Princess of Wales, a photograph of West Ham football team and one of darts player Eric Bristow, whose skills are rarely matched by the darts players here.

There have been changes among those pulling the Luxford and Copley beer pumps and filling glasses from the optics. After the Watts, the Butchers took over as landlords, then Sharon and Simon Wicks hoped to be granted the tenancy but Eddie Royle was the successful applicant. Now Sharon is back. But Pat Butcher has her sights set on winning back the licence.

The beer is good stuff and customers can expect their drinks to be freshly pulled. (In *Coronation Street*'s Rovers Return the glasses are often half-filled already!) But woe betide the drinker who asks for a pint or three of low-alcohol beer. Because this television pub is actually a studio set and doesn't have a cellar, low-alcohol beer drawn from a barrel under the counter would fill the pub with froth, so it's the same beer that comes from the other pump.

How much is drunk in The Vic? Quite a lot – but a real publican would not be happy. Too many of the regulars drink only soft drinks. The gin and tonics are all tonic and even the biggest boozer, Pete Beale, drinks only lemonade. That's the reason he has a special pewter tankard – so we don't spot that it's not beer he's knocking back. The tankard, though, is so famous that actor Peter Dean reports it has been pinched twice and he has had to replace it on both occasions.

The pub grub is always changing. Ethel, Mags, Kathy, Mo and Ian have all been seen to prepare it and, like the café food, the crew make sure it doesn't go to waste when the director calls 'Its a wrap!'

TheVic

Apparently an efficient barmaid, Mo Butcher was really no such thing. Edna Dore, who played her, revealed she was always having to do retakes because 'I made the till drawer shoot out unexpectedly! Nick Berry, who played Wicksy, showed me what to do, but I still got it wrong.'

Leslie Grantham, Mike Reid and Pam St Clement all have painful memories of the bar, too. Pam said 'It's worse than being behind the bar for real, because in the show you have to stand there, often at an angle, so the cameras can catch you and whoever is on the other side of the bar. And if it's not your storyline, you're there simply as furniture. You have to hold a certain position while they check the lighting or whatever.

'Mike ended up with major surgery on his spine – I was so worried for him. And I had to have regular physiotherapy. I still have it.'

There have been all sorts of parties and knees-ups in The Vic bar. None have been melodious. Not Wicksy's piano playing (a skilled bit of faking by Nick Berry). Not the charity nights, the drag nights, not the Karaoke on New Year's Eve 1990 when Pauline was Dolly Parton, Arthur was Kenny Rogers and Eddie sang 'Blue Velvet'.

Perhaps the most disastrous party was the Christmas dinner at which Den presented Angie with their divorce papers. The kitchen upstairs has seen a bucketful of misery too. Remember Angie's suicide attempt?

There is another thing which makes The Vic special – the carpet. Infertility experts should perhaps study it. Michelle, and then Cindy, needed to try it for one night only. Result, two new citizens. Perhaps it's magic?

The Market

Like long-established street markets all over Britain, Bridge Street Market, off Albert Square, is a medley of stalls and pitches: a noisy, colourful collection of goods to buy and people to meet. The stall-holders, the goods and the customers change but the friendly bustle remains the same.

This market has already survived one major council development plan, thanks to Pete Beale's determination to fight for the fruit and vegetable pitch that has been the sole Beale family asset for years. Everyone in the family has earned a little money serving on it, too. April and her husband, Greg Mackintosh – they sold crockery – joined him. So did fat Lil, who has a clothes stall: Tracy, who sells flowers and helps behind the bar at The Vic on occasions; Maude, who has a paperback book stall; Sadie, who sells china; Billy, who sells shirts; and Lou Gold, who sells luggage (when not assisted by Trevor Short, who used to let

people walk away with a lot of it). Kathy sold her knitted jumpers there, Cindy and her mum their colourful hats, Barry Clark (and sometimes Rod) sold records and tapes.

There's always a mate around to mind your stall while you nip off for a break. If none of the family is within shouting distance, Pete might call on the services of Big Ron, who runs the hardware stall, if he isn't in the pub drinking away his profits. Or his pal, Jackie Stone, who used to sell bric-a-brac. It was among his 'treasures', remember, that Sharon found Den's signet ring, which led to the discovery of Den's body in the canal. And Ulric, the cheerful West Indian, sells his second-hand records, so there is usually a reggae beat pounding away in the background.

Charlie Cotton, too, was known to try his luck with suitcases full of fluffy animals, wind-up toys, playing cards – anything he thought would earn him a few dishonest quid. There's a shoe stall near the Turpin Road end of the market and a clothes stall near the café, where Mary used to buy a few items with money she'd

Top left: **Bridge Street Market.**
Inset: **Cindy on her hat stall.**
Below left: **Kathy selling her jumpers.** *Below:* **Pete Beale.**

probably wheedled out of men the night before.

But because Bridge Street Market isn't quite like others, only coming alive on location days, the props people have special tasks to perform. One is to keep the clothes and goods up to date. Keen-eyed viewers write to tell the producers if particular 'lines' have been on sale too long, just as they often write in begging to be able to buy various things they see on the screen. A hat on Cindy's stall caught one woman's fancy. She said she'd pay the asking price; it matched the dress she planned to wear for her son's wedding. Alas, she was politely told she'd have to look elsewhere.

Another task is gently to stop the cast and crew helping themselves to the apples and pears temptingly piled up on Pete's stall. Fresh supplies are brought in each week, with the props department taking care that the fruit and veg will still be in season six weeks later when the scenes are screened. They tried to use fake fruit at one stage, but Peter Dean, who plays Pete and has sold fruit on a real market stall, said it felt and looked quite wrong in the brown paper bags.

Little is wasted, though. Items which aren't likely to last for the next session in front of the cameras are removed and delivered to folk in a nearby sheltered housing block. Equally, food prepared for the café scenes never remains on the plates or in the saucepans once the scene has been successfully shot. The cast and crew descend on it like locusts, so not a baked bean or a slice of toast remains.

Are you an Albert Square expert?

ANSWERS ON PAGE 128

1 Who gave Lofty guitar lessons?

2 What did Kelvin give Ian for his eighteenth birthday?

3 Where was Pete the night Kathy was raped?

4 Who accompanied Kathy to the police station to make a statement?

5 Who found Lou Beale's body?

6 With which two people did Lou leave instructions for her funeral?

7 Which friend of Darren's put a crooked BMW car dealer on to Frank Butcher?

8 Why did Ethel decide not to marry Benny Bloom?

9 On the run in Manchester, Den stayed with a woman. What was her name?

10 Which of his fellow prison inmates lied so Den would be beaten up?

1 Who punched a fist through the glass of The Queen Vic's door?

2 How was Michelle earning the money to buy a motor bike?

3 Arthur had just been made redundant from what job?

4 Where did Pauline and Arthur go looking for Mark on New Year's Eve?

5 Where was Mark working when he was found?

6 Why was Martin's christening postponed?

7 Debs was worried to find Mary working at slave-wage rates on what?

8 What was Den selling, which had 'fallen off the back of a lorry', in December?

9 Which member of the Fowler family lives at Leigh-on-Sea?

10 Which schoolgirl asked Dr Legg to put her on the pill?

1 Who was the host of *Cat and Mouse*, the TV quiz show in which Arthur appeared?

2 Where had Paul Priestley and Trevor Short first met?

3 What was the name of the estate agent selling Doris' bed and breakfast house?

4 Where did Julie first plan to site her hairdressing salon?

5 What did those premises become?

6 From what job was Sharon sacked?

7 What did Charlie buy Dot before he vanished from the scene?

8 What did Matthew Jackson do for a living?

9 Who went sleepwalking in The Queen Vic?

10 What did Cindy deliberately drop into Wicksy's pocket?

1 Who played The Black Death in the Walford Carnival?

2 Name the knitting firm set up by Lofty and Kelvin.

3 What colour was Simon Wicks' sports car?

4 Name the male stripper who appeared at The Queen Vic's Ladies' Night.

5 Which football team does Arthur support?

6 Who tried unsuccessfully to pull Pete Beale up on a platform to perform with him during The Vic's Drag Night?

7 What did the Osmans pay for Den's Rover?

8 Where did Roy Quick take Debs Wilkins for a night out?

9 Why did the Carpenters refuse to talk to the Fowlers?

10 Why did Tom Clements steal Arthur's prize leeks?

1 Who turned up late at Pauline and Arthur's twenty-fifth wedding anniversary party?

2 Who called off a feud specially for the occasion?

3 What did Ian throw through the window of Cindy's parents' cottage?

4 Who helped Nick try to poison Dot?

5 Where did Pauline Fowler find a full-time job?

6 With whom and where did Sharon spend Christmas?

7 Where does Mo Butcher's daughter, Joan, live?

8 Why did Lloyd Tavernier secretly borrow his grand-dad Jules' bicycle?

9 What was the resulting effect on his health?

10 How did Kendle at the Council try to bribe Pete to drop his opposition to the market closure?

1 What business did Ali and Mehmet's father run?

2 What is little Vicki's middle name?

3 What did Barry Clark sell on his stall?

4 Who was the first to find Pat Wicks after she'd been attacked?

5 Where did The Vic's Ladies' Darts Team have their first away match?

6 What did Ethel give Vicki as a first birthday present?

7 Who lost his family home in a poker game?

8 Who or what was Dog Market?

9 Who or what was Crush?

10 What happened each time Mags tried to buy a home in Albert Square?

1 Where does Eddie Royle's friend, Eibhlin, work?

2 What's the name of Rachel's former boyfriend?

3 To which hospital was Eddie taken after Grant attacked him?

4 Which policeman questioned Sharon about the attack on Eddie?

5 What does Kevin, the man in Peggy Mitchell's life, run?

6 Which young woman from Celestine's church was besotted with him?

7 Who introduced Michelle to the time share work?

8 What is the name of Ian's catering business?

9 Disa O'Brian's younger sister was also abused by their stepfather. What is her name?

10 What did Ian 'plant' in The Dagmar so he could tip off the police about it?

The real Murderers of Eddie Royle

The Walford police will tell you the deceased was stabbed once. The truth is he died of multiple wounds. He was the victim of a vicious gang who, in the spring of 1991 and in cold blood, plotted the death of one of the best-respected and most hard-working citizens of Albert Square. His name was Eddie Royle.

A confession has been made by one of them, under duress. *EastEnders'* storyline editor Andrew Holden does not look like a man with blood on his hands. He has an alibi for that September night – he was at home, babysitting. His small daughter will confirm it. Yet he is guilty.

Eddie had never done Andrew Holden any harm. He had never done anyone any harm even if Sharon Watts, whom he sacked, mightn't see it that way. He was due to marry the beautiful colleen he loved and perhaps in time to make his old dad, John, a happy grand-dad. Those were some of the reasons the knife went in, Holden says. The others were that he was good-looking, single and his name wasn't Beale or Fowler.

What's more, Holden, thirty-five, admits he enjoyed the 'crime'. They all did. Proud of the shock it caused, the mystery, the upset to so many other characters it has provoked. He asks for another death, that of Charlie Cotton only a few months earlier, to be taken into consideration. He shows no remorse and will not promise never to take another soap life. Because, you see, he and his colleagues are serial killers.

'Actually, we wanted to kill him earlier,' said bookish, quietly-spoken Holden, who came to *EastEnders* eighteen months ago after 'playing God' in a similar way behind the scenes at *Emmerdale*, Yorkshire Television's country soap opera.

They wanted to do something to remind people that *EastEnders* is not like other series.

It's unpredictable and dangerous. They had a motive – population control.

'There are practical restrictions on the size of the cast. It was becoming impossible to provide good stories for all of the regulars, to give them something that's unique. When you have a lot of single people you cannot keep them alive simply by writing about the businesses they're in. We could do it with Ian Beale – but it has been a problem for others, for Kathy, for example. So something has got to give.'

When well-known and well-liked characters leave soap operas rumours fly that there has been a row which the actor lost or that the series' bosses believe the character was boring or the actor was boring. None of those reasons applied here.

'When you begin to talk about a character leaving, the best of all worlds is that it's voluntary on the part of the actor. If not, you must play God but you try to do it in a responsible way, not like little boys pulling the wings off a fly,' Holden explains.

So one of Albert Square's single residents was being stalked. Why not Pete Beale?

'Some characters are almost synonymous with the programme because they have been there since Day One. They carry a lot of history. Original characters are very precious things. That wasn't the case with Eddie. Eddie was not organic to the programme: we portrayed him as a man still having great difficulty coming to terms with the history of the pub he ran and the people around it.

Facing page: **Eddie Royle was a marked man long before the story editor had him murdered.**

Above: **Pete is 'an untouchable'.**

'The people very close to Eddie were also itinerant characters. He was not married to Kathy, she was not carrying his child.

'Pete is different. He has always seen himself as a family man and in the future we may see him making a determined effort to put his family back together. Whatever happens he'll always carry a torch for Kathy.'

There were other motives, too. 'We were also looking at Sharon's long-term future and, because she's Angie and Den's daughter, it seemed right that she should succeed them, at least for a time, in running The Vic. We also looked at Pat and wondered if she was really enjoying the B & B. It seemed a good idea for her to return behind the bar, for there to be some friction between her and Sharon and difficulties between Frank and Pat.'

For all these things to happen Eddie Royle had to die. But first, life had to seem full of promise for the poor devil. He and Eibhlin happily made plans. Then this tragedy!

Holden confesses that the crime was his idea originally. But he could not do it alone. He had to discuss it with two script editors, two story editors, two producers and the executive producer. In all there were eight 'murderers'.

'Having taken this decision to prune for the health of the programme, what you want is a good story and we all believed it to be a good story, there were no disagreements. Our discussions were still extremely fraught because we had to be absolutely certain it was the right thing to do. The questions were then of timing – for the actor and the audience.'

They decided to commit the crime in July, with the scenes being screened in September. That meant this strong story about what had actually happened would run up to Christmas.

'It's not a whodunnit, we're not teasing the audience. But it is a mystery and I think it becomes gripping and exciting.'

Andrew Holden does not deny that his idea created many painful problems for others.

'I know that Michael Melia, the actor who played Eddie, was surprised and disappointed because he has invested a great deal in Eddie, as had the audience. That's why the story worked so well.'

Outsiders sometimes believe that once actors become part of a long-running series they're *in* for ever. But the reality is they're

part of the ebb and flow of the story and contracts tend to be short-term for all actors.

Before that fateful night for Eddie Royle, Dot's husband Charlie's lorry was involved in a crash. Charlie Cotton died. Andrew Holden confesses to causing that crash. Again, he conspired with the 'gang'. But what Dot and Nick don't know is that he did it for them.

He explains: 'We wanted to bring Nick Cotton back and we also wanted to push Dot forward and change her life. But the problem was how? The last time we saw Nick he had been attempting to kill his mother. Dot isn't a fool so we knew getting them back together was like a three card trick. How do we get out of this? So we made him a heroin addict. That made him vulnerable, in a mess and needing his mother to get money for him.

'We then had to kill Charlie because I figured that only in a state of shock and uncertainty about her belief in God would Dot contemplate forgiving Nick and attempting to reform him.

'She decides to believe that she can make a decent human being of Nick. She feels it's her last chance. As a widow Dot enters new territory. Dot's snobbery is based on ludicrous misconceptions, one of which is that she is better than Ethel because she has a husband. She is going to have a lot of scope working in the B & B. Dot's life is going to change.'

June Brown is one of many members of the cast who care passionately about their characters and, like Dot Cotton, she had to have her say. In some cases actors can influence the fate of their characters. Usually they cannot.

'I was very unhappy to learn that Charlie would be killed off,' she said. 'I would have preferred it if they'd left the door open for him possibly to turn up again one day. I went to see the writers and put this forward. I suggested that there could be some uncertainty about

the body. Charlie may have picked up a hitch-hiker and he was the one who died. John Altman, who plays Nick, was also sorry about Charlie. We weren't thinking just about Christopher Hancock, who played Charlie so well, it was that we liked the character and it seemed a waste. But I was too late, I couldn't change their minds.

'In the past I have talked things through and I was listened to. I felt that something planned for Dot concerning Mo didn't make sense and four scenes were re-written.

As for Dot's son Nick, June said she much prefers John Altman, the actor who plays him. 'He's well-mannered, he's definitely got class. He's a very well-brought-up boy!' she joked.

'There is a lot of comedy in *EastEnders*, although it's not the safe sort. It has a crueller, blacker sense of humour than old ladies nattering in a pub,' says Andrew Holden.

Nevertheless, none of the 'gang' are laughing about the murder of Eddie Royle. 'It was a relatively clean and unmessy operation, though', he says in their defence.

Propping up the Set

When Ian Beale wrote off his van and Mark Fowler wrecked his motor bike things weren't as bad as they seemed. Props buyer Monica Boggust assures anyone concerned about the money involved that special already-wrecked vehicles are bought for those scenes and then returned to the scrap-yard after shooting. Ian's van was a heap costing one hundred pounds.

The raffia donkey that Angie and Sharon Watts brought home to Walford from their holiday in Spain really came from a tea shop in Dorchester. And just in the nick of time.

Monica had almost to admit defeat after five days of frantic searching for the souvenir everyone associates with Spanish holidays but which has actually gone out of fashion with travellers because it's too big and bulky.

'We needed a new one, which meant we didn't want to hire a used donkey from a theatrical props supplier. The Spanish Tourist Board told us of a Products From Spain Shop but they had none. Then a woman customer in that shop, who'd overheard the telephone conversation, went back to tell them she'd seen one in a National Trust tea shop in Dorchester. They rang us back, we rang the tea shop in Dorchester and they said it wasn't their tea shop but one down the road. We rang that one and the kind lady still had one. She rushed out, wrapped it up and put it on an overnight train. We collected it from the station early in the morning and used it that morning on the set.'

IT'S ONLY MAKE BELIEVE–BUT EVEN SO...

The *EastEnders* cast and production team believe the show has some of the most warm-hearted viewers ever. When Wicksy was saving up to buy a new car, for instance, a young fan sent him five pounds towards it – the money was sent on to a charity. When Arthur had his nervous breakdown, several kind viewers wrote in, offering to tend his allotment until he was better. Well-wishers have sent generous gifts for the babies. They offer advice to the characters over their problems and confide in them about their own.

But *EastEnders* must have some of the cheekiest fans too. Several of the cast have received marriage proposals, along with suggestions of other leisure activities that have even brought blushes to the cheeks of Mike Reid and Leslie Grantham. One actress received an artfully painted

Is she Sophie or really Diane?

watercolour portrait from an admiring fan. It was a direct and unusual way of introducing himself – the painting was not of his face but of a part of the anatomy not normally painted on its own.

Some viewers reprimanded the actors for their characters' actions. Sophie Lawrence was yanked by the arm by a concerned lady who held on to her while trying to telephone the police to say she'd found 'that runaway teenager who was such a worry to her family'. Another woman, who disliked gay men, chased actor Gary Hailes, who isn't gay but played Barry Clark who was, around a supermarket brandishing a stick of French bread at him.

Gary also suffered more severely from prejudice against gays: someone actually attacked him. A man saw him when he was buying petrol at a filling station. Gary got into his car and pulled out but the man came after him, opened his car door and tried to strangle him, shouting 'You effing poof! I hate you.' After he left the series, Gary lost a job as a presenter of a children's show because of the gay tag.

But then no one said acting in a controversial drama series like *EastEnders* was easy.

But the second time a raffia donkey was required, Monica was inundated with them. An appeal on Radio Bedford brought a donkey stampede: the station received 460 calls.

Finding furniture to suit the *EastEnders* characters and keeping within strict budgets means Monica and her team have to be crafty. Den's up-market mistress, Jan, may have had a stylish flat with stylish sofas, but what few viewers realised was that Jan's furniture was handed down to her rival, Den's wife Angie, when she moved into a flat in The Dagmar.

Then after the fire in The Dagmar, the sofas were re-covered for the Karims. When Rachel Kominsky moved into their house, the rooms were empty – but look whose sofa, re-covered yet again, has pride of place in the living room now! Similarly, Colin Russell's couch now lives in Grant Mitchell's flat.

Other props have become jokes on the set. The washing twirling round in the six fully functioning machines in Dot's launderette is not a selection of the cast's smalls, as has sometimes been suggested. But it *is* the same washing that has been there since February 1985. On the other hand, when Dot accidentally dyed the white sheets from Pat's B & B pink, after washing them with a red sock, they were white sheets specially bought and genuinely tinted that way.

The cast's favourite props are the special occasion cakes. Usually there have to be six of these to account for retakes of the scenes where an actor or actress cuts the first slice. Wendy Richard favours fruit cake and the baker is always gratified to hear that as soon as the scenes are completed, the cast and crew make sure there's never a crumb left.

Life in the launderette.

Finding the Faces and Places

The sixty or so people who work on *EastEnders* at any one time can change and control most things to make the show look right. But when it comes to the weather, they must often give in to the elements.

Standing out in windy Albert Square is a job for those with good circulation and an ever-ready range of thermal underwear. Peter Dean, who plays stall-holder Pete Beale and actually comes from a long line of costermongers, knows a few tricks for keeping warm. One is to line his shoes with newspaper. Wendy Richard, long ago decided that however bulky they make her appear, she'll wear up to three vests and pairs of long-johns rather than freeze. Our quick-changing climate causes frequent continuity problems. More than once, the local fire brigade has been called to remove snow from the roofs of houses in the Square because the scenes shot the day before show blue skies, and the sudden appearance of the snow would baffle viewers.

Delaying outdoor filming in the hope that temperatures will rise can be risky. When it came to shooting the Walford Easter Carnival, producer Corinne Hollingworth was easily persuaded to postpone filming in what turned out to be a bitterly cold February. 'We delayed for four weeks, but we ended up doing it on one of the coldest days of the year. We had to give the actors constant hot drinks and have teams standing by with warm overcoats, whipping them off at the last minute,' she said.

Then there was the carefully prepared Love In The Graveyard incident which became a wash-out. The setting for the romantic scene where Sam Mitchell and Ricky Butcher defied her mother's ban to meet was to be a cemetery. Props boss Monica Boggust knew it would offend some viewers if the young lovers were seen frolicking near recognisable tombstones, so a special fake graveyard was arranged by the researchers and designers.

Corinne Hollingworth lamented: 'We were able to film earlier scenes on a day of lovely sunshine but the ones which were to come immediately afterwards, on the same day in the graveyard, we filmed on the following Tuesday. It was pouring with rain. We decided that however besotted with each other these kids were, they'd never lie down on soaking wet gravestones in order to be together. So the whole scene was switched to inside Ricky's camper van at the last minute.'

The actors themselves accept these alterations stoically. They also accept that there are things they mustn't change without consultation. One is the length and colour of their hair: there's a 'hair clause' in their contracts. So Sid Owen could not simply rush out and have a short back and sides haircut if he felt like it. Sue Tully, who did have her hair cut very short, had to wait until the storyline had Michelle feeling fed up with her appearance and deciding on a 'new look'. June Brown enjoys Dot Cotton's out-of-date 'Italian Boy' hairstyle and frumpy clothes. But the actress had long yearned to improve her prominent front teeth. Expensive tooth capping would be something Dot could not afford, she was told. Early in 1991, though, June's teeth became loose. There was no alternative. June and Dot now look more glamorous.

Once *EastEnders* became a success, it was never hard to find good actors who wanted to join the cast. What has been hard, though, has been finding 'families'; combinations of performers who look and sound as though they could be related. It has given the two *EastEnders* producers, Corinne Hollingworth and Pat Sandys, many headaches.

'The most difficult job we've had was finding six black actors who fitted the bill for the Tavernier family,' said Corinne. 'Here we needed two teenagers who looked around fifteen but were actually older, had left school and had mature attitudes to work. They had to love music, hanging around in tracksuits and, most important, they had to look as if they could be twins. And for Clyde, we needed someone who looked as though he'd been a boxer but also seemed thoughtful.

'To cast Phil and Grant Mitchell, we saw lots of actors and we screen-tested them together. There were some good actors we had to turn down because we couldn't find the right 'brother'. When it came to casting their sister, Sam, it was easier because we'd decided

Gillian Taylforth is well wrapped up.
Facing page: **Ricky and Sam together.**

Facing page: Once upon a time the Beales were a close-knit family who helped each other out on their market stall. Now, times have changed and so have attitudes. Kathy's rape by James Willmott-Brown and Ian's change of personality from kind young man to ruthless tycoon, have fractured and frayed Beale family ties. Life for them will never be the same again.

They may not always be a happy family but the Fowlers have stuck together during the upheavals of the past few years. They weathered the storms of Mark being in a detention centre, Michelle having Den Watts' baby and Arthur's breakdown and subsequent imprisonment, and now must face up to the worries and uncertainty over Mark, who is HIV positive.

Life in Bridge Street Market has always been colourful to say the least. Stall-holders have come and gone, but Pete Beale *(above)* continues with his fruit and veg stall. *Right:* Sue and Ali Osman ran the café during its greasy-spoon days but problems eventually took their toll on the combustible marriage. *Facing page:* He's now won the contract to keep up the Square's gardens, but several of his neighbours really feel that Arthur Fowler just dreams his days away. At least his heart's in the right place.

Facing page: **Despite his philanderings, his tough guy attitude and all their sexual problems, Angie never stopped loving Den - not even in the face of his affair with Miss Silk Knickers, as she called his mistress, Jan Hammond** *(above).*

on Steve and Ross and we knew the sort of round, open face we needed. We saw Danniella (Westbrook) first and liked her, then saw some others, but came back to her.

'Finding the right man to play Eddie was hard because someone of that age, about forty-five, brings a lot of background and personality with him. We needed an actor who seemed strong because he was supposed to have been a policeman. And he was taking over that place behind the bar that Leslie Grantham and Mike Reid had held. Michael (Melia) struck us as an expansive sort who also had a bit of a twinkle.'

Perhaps the casting decision most agonised over was that of hiring Todd Carty for the role David Scarboro had filled before his death. 'We felt it was dishonest to suggest that Pauline Fowler would not have cared where her son was, so we started looking for a new Mark and were extremely lucky with Todd Carty. The audience knew him from *Grange Hill* and he was just right,' said Corinne.

But they did not tell Todd then, or any of the other actors auditioned, that this character would be revealed as having a terrifying illness. Actors really are kept in the dark about what will happen to them in their 'other lives'.

Story editor Andrew Holden recalled: 'It was a very fraught time but we decided we had to make sense of Mark's story. There was so much that hadn't been explained because of David's death. We needed a powerful reason to bring him home and we decided to make him HIV positive. The idea was greeted with immediate enthusiasm. I suppose it was because the script team are relatively young and lots of us knew someone who was suffering in this way. Also it did seem that public opinion had gone through the hysteria stage over Aids and it was becoming a fact of life. But it still went against the grain to do this to

Above: Mark and Gill are both HIV positive.
Facing page: It took time to cast the complete Tavernier (bottom left) and Mitchell families.

our young romantic lead!'

It was a decision that many people were to applaud. These included the Terence Higgins Trust counsellors who advised Todd and the writers about the problems of people coping with being HIV positive; doctors working in this field and hoping to spread the message that everyone is now at risk; and also the Government's Chief Medical Officer at the Department of Health, Sir Donald Acheson.

He wrote personally to the production team in February 1991 to congratulate and thank them for the 'sensible and sensitive' storyline. 'I am informed that the National Aids Helplines have been inundated with calls triggered directly by the programme', he wrote. 'I have little doubt that the programme will be of immense help.'

Albert Square Year by Year

FEBRUARY

Reg Cox, who has been missing for three days, is found dead in his armchair when Den, Ali and Arthur break down his door. Det. Sgt Rich isn't convinced the death is due to natural causes. Dr Legg confirms Pauline's pregnancy, but when Lou hears the news she's furious and orders her daughter to 'get rid of it'; she won't have a baby in *her* house. Jobless Arthur is offered a few weeks' work by builder Tony Carpenter. Sue and Ali Osman at the café start up a Golden Circle

Sue Osman outside Ali's Café.

money chain letter. Den, when not phoning his mistress, Jan, is ducking and diving and following up one dodgy deal or another. When Nick Cotton argues with Ali about Reg Cox, Den bans them both from the pub.

Nick scrounging off Dot again.

MARCH

Michelle and her best friend, Sharon, compete to go out with Kelvin Carpenter. Det. Sgt Rich quizzes Lofty about the Luftwaffe badge Mark gave him. It brings on one of Lofty's asthma attacks. Mary and baby Annie move into Reg's room. Heroin addict Nick Cotton is stopped by Ethel from persuading Mary to go on the game, so she takes up embroidery at slave wage rates instead. Racist slogans are painted on the front of the foodstore, handiwork of members of the New Movement that Nick wants Lofty and Mark to join. It earns Nick a walloping from Tony.

APRIL

Naima confides to Pauline that she doesn't sleep with Saeed. Pete teases Ian about his cooking. He tells his gran he's unhappy but Kathy, his mum, reacts angrily when Lou offers advice. He also tells of the part Nick and Mark played in the attack on the foodstore. Nick Cotton's arrest is reported. Pauline packs Lou and Michelle off to Clacton. Mark runs away. Debs begins a Save Our Square campaign after hearing of a redevelopment threat. Angie discovers that Den, in Spain, is with another woman,

Tony Carpenter ready for action.

probably Jan. Hurt, she retaliates by seducing Tony. Michelle and Lou return from Clacton, with Michelle fantasising about a waiter called Carlo.

Angie, Den and Sharon Watts.

MAY

Ian takes over cooking the snacks at The Vic and plans a party. With Kelvin, he teases Michelle by inviting a 'Carlo' – really their pal Spotty. Sharon realises what's happening between Tony and her mother. Angie tells her about her dad's jaunt with Jan. When Den returns, they agree to end their affairs and try again but a night in the same bed is a failure. Mary's anxious father, Chris, arrives. Dr Legg is busy: Lou has shingles; Arthur is depressed at not finding any work; Sharon wants to go on the pill (to tempt Kelvin). Then Pauline has a bad turn and is taken to hospital.

JUNE

Lou stays with Pete and Kathy for a while; they find it a strain. Tony is upset to see Sharon wearing the bracelet he gave to Angie as a love token and snubs Angie the next time he sees her. Kelvin and Michelle split up. Unhappy Sharon complains to her mother about her heavy drinking, then steals some gin and gets drunk herself. Ali stakes his café and car in a poker game but wins. Before he and Sue can enjoy his luck they find their baby Hassan has died in his cot in the night. They take him to Andy, who is a nurse, but it's too late to revive him. Lofty and Michelle help them out by running the café.

Guizin Osman comforts Sue.

JULY

The Osman funeral takes place. Sue is numb. Dot Cotton, Pauline's partner at the launderette, turns up late, upset about the gossip circulating about her Nick, who is due in court. He gets off, with probation. Michelle streaks Lofty's hair and it ends up green. Couples are arguing: Saeed with Naima about her sex ban; Angie with Den because not drinking makes her nervy; and Kathy with Pete because having Lou to stay is a strain. When Lou hears that Michelle has moved into her room, she insists on returning home to reclaim it. She loans Michelle money for a motor bike. Ian and Kelvin go into the knitting business together.

AUGUST

Pauline has a baby boy – Martin. Dr Legg thrusts Mary's little Annie into Sue's arms and Sue starts to grieve properly. She takes Hassan's clothes in a Tesco carrier bag to a none-too-delighted Pauline. At Charity Night at The Vic, Angie is drinking heavily again and tries to auction her underwear. Den books her into a health farm. Pete accuses Arthur of being lazy. Mary tells Pauline she can't read and that she's up in court for shop-lifting. Michelle, peeved about her baby brother and her father's new job as a cleaner at her school, starts going out at night and drinking. She has a couple of after-hours chats with Den. One night, unseen by anyone, they make love.

SEPTEMBER

Someone is sending poison pen letters. Baby Martin has gastro-enteritis and his christening is postponed. Sharon, upset about her parents' quarrelling, flirts with Lofty. Den is furious and hits her. Nick Cotton returns and Ethel locks herself indoors in fear. Michelle confides to Lou she's pregnant and a test confirms it. She refuses to name the father. Soon everyone is discussing what to do about it. Andy gives Debs two kittens to make up for the fact that after they were burgled he found he'd forgotten to renew their insurance policy.

Pauline in the launderette.

OCTOBER

Michelle arranges to meet the father of her unborn child by the canal. It's Den and she tells him she won't have an abortion. Simon Wicks, Pete's son from his first marriage, arrives, upsetting Kathy and Ian. He offers to move on. There have been break-ins at the launderette and Dr Legg's surgery; Kathy's medical notes are missing. Saeed plans to sell up and return to Bangladesh. Nick tells Kathy he knows she had

Den's to be a father.

a baby when she was fourteen and demands money to keep quiet. Sheena Mennell, Mary's stripper friend, persuades her to take up stripping. Martin is christened, with Wicksy standing in for Den as a godfather.

NOVEMBER

Mary begins work as a stripper. Sheena babysits Annie one night but abandons her when she picks up a man. Sue rescues the child. Nick blackmails Kathy again. Angie tells Den that she wants to meet Jan, her rival. Ian prepares for a boxing match and he wins, thanks to Pete's encouragement and Wicksy's

coaching. Lou keeps falling over and seems unwell. Kelvin's hopes for a reconciliation between his parents are dashed when his mother, Hannah, reveals there's another man, Neville, in her life. The men in the Square debate suitable punishments for Nick over his behaviour to Kathy.

DECEMBER

The thief at The Vic turns out to be Sharon. Angie drives Den's car to a darts match but she and it come home the worse for wear at 3 a.m. Lou, home from

hospital, is grumpy about sleeping downstairs and using a commode. Pete makes things worse by telling her she's now past working on the stall. Saeed is in the audience when Mary strips – he's lonely because Naima wants a divorce. Debs and Andy get engaged. On Boxing Day Cassie Carpenter turns up at her father's house, covered in bruises; Neville has been hitting her. After Christmas, Arthur and Pauline hear that Mark is in Southend. They track him down, and find him living with a woman whose two kids call him 'Daddy'.

A troubled Den has a chat with newcomer Simon Wicks.

JANUARY

While he looks for the man who mugged her, Det. Sgt Roy Quick seems to be falling for Debs. Andy is soon jealous. Pauline brings

Long-suffering Andy O'Brien.

home a stray dog which causes havoc. Angie is fined two hundred and fifty pounds for her driving offence. Ali fears he's impotent. Two local thugs, Beresford and Vic, offer Naima and Sue 'protection' at the shop and café. When Tony hears of it, he thumps Beresford. Angie and Sharon try to persuade Den to attend marriage guidance, but he plans to see Jan and asks Pete to provide him with an alibi. Cassie suffers a broken arm – is this more of Neville's violence?

FEBRUARY

There's a drag artist at a stag night at The Vic and Jan turns up to talk things out with Den. In the morning she and Angie meet in a park. Eventually Den says he's moving into a bedsit, but he lies – he's with Jan. Lofty proposes to Michelle but she turns him down. A couple of heavies are watching Wicksy. Eventually he tells Lou he's involved with loan sharks because he inherited debts from a band he played with. Pete lends him the money Kathy and Ian wanted for a car so he can pay them off. Ethel's pug Willie disappears.

MARCH

Angie gathers together a pile of sleeping pills and washes them down with gin. Den, who has argued with Jan, returns to The Vic kitchen in time to find her and have her rushed to hospital where her stomach is pumped out. Her friends take turns to watch her. Den, guilt-ridden, is attentive. Much to Dot's delight, her husband Charlie turns up, but he upsets her by stealing from her and leaving. Andy helps Mary with reading lessons. For once she doesn't wear her mask of make-up, but she's confused to find he doesn't fancy her. Roy Quick is Ethel's hero when he finds the man who has Willie. He also proposes to Debs.

APRIL

Angie and Den depart for a holiday in Ibiza but Den is soon flying home alone. Angie stays on to drink and flirt. Michelle says 'yes' to Lofty and Ian begins to date Sharon. Arthur starts

Lofty and Michelle get engaged, but Den bought the ring.

the ill-fated Christmas Club fund. Hannah and Cassie leave Neville and move in with Tony. Debt-ridden Debs has to show the DHSS she's not co-habiting with Andy, so lodger Naima has the main bedroom, Andy the spare room and Debs a camp bed. Den is relieved to provide Lofty with a ring for Michelle but angry to find Ian necking with Sharon. Angie, meanwhile, hooks Andy, her new conquest.

MAY

Kathy quits her job in disgust when Angie tells of her new affair. Debs takes over. Sue tells everyone she's pregnant. Mehmet joins Ali

in a minicab venture, called Ozcabs, with an old Cortina. Dot wins two hundred and fifty pounds at bingo then 'loses' her cheque book after Nick reappears. Lofty fails a medical to become a traffic warden. Andy arranges a washing-up job at the hospital for Mary. Sharon hides from her parents at Mary's. Michelle is rushed to hospital and gives birth to Vicki. Den dares to visit and holds the baby.

JUNE

Pat Wicks turns up and tells Pete that Wicksy is not his son, although Lou later insists that he is. New mum Michelle, Sharon and

Ian all take school exams. Andy splits from Angie and gets back with Debs after she says 'no' to Quick. Den sells his dodgy Rover car to Ozcabs. Kelvin and Harry and Tessa, his friends from college, plan to form a band with Wicksy. Wicksy brings in his punk friend Eddie and they both audition. There's a burglary at Dr Legg's and Ethel's and Lofty's flats are raided too. Sharon agrees to be bridesmaid and Wicksy best man at the wedding of Michelle and Lofty, but Arthur is fretting about how to pay for it.

JULY

Pauline and Kathy go to creative art classes, which both Arthur and Pete think means drawing nude men. Dot consults Dr Legg about her hot flushes and funny turns. Sue learns she isn't pregnant after all. Quick suspects Kelvin of being the burglar because he's black. Debs puts rat poison down in the shop – it explains why Roly, Den and Angie's poodle, is suddenly ill. Mark turns up with his friend, Owen, who shares joints with Kelvin and, to Tony's horror, Cassie. The Carpenters won't speak to the Fowlers because of it.

Pat Wicks arrives in the Square and makes a few things clear.

After a terrible gig, The Banned live up to their name.

AUGUST

Sharon announces she's leaving school and Hannah wants Cassie to go to a boarding school. Andy and Debs argue about his lending money to Wicksy. Then, seeing a lorry veer out of control, Andy dives to save a small boy who is in the road and is killed himself. Debs is comforted to learn that Andy carried a donor card and his kidneys saved someone's life. Colin moves into the Carpenter's top flat. After a shambles of a gig, the band, now called The Banned, are banned from The Vic. Mehmet spikes Mary's drink because he believes she told his wife, Guizin, that they've slept together.

SEPTEMBER

Dithery Dot is arrested for shop-lifting. Sue and Ali discuss adopting a baby from Cyprus. Cassie runs away from school but Kelvin persuades her to go back. Pauline wins a Glamorous Granny competition. As wedding presents begin to arrive at the Fowlers', Lofty reads *The Joy of Sex*. There is no joy for Arthur who confesses to Pauline that he used the Christmas Club's fifteen hundred pounds to pay for Michelle's wedding. After riotous stag and hen parties, the couple dress up and go to the church, but Michelle can't go through with the wedding. Lofty seems calm, but then breaks down.

OCTOBER

Tom, Den's potman, wins the prize for the best leeks at the produce show. Actually, he stole them from Arthur. Ethel slips and breaks a hip so Pauline takes over her cleaning job; Colin asks her to 'do' for him too. He invites Debs in for a drink and she flirts with him.

Lofty is left in the lurch.

Angie taking Den for a ride in more ways than one.

Pat arrives, claiming that her husband beat her up and threw her out. Angie gives her a job at The Vic. Kathy decides to try a knitting venture and takes a market pitch. She also tries to help Angie, who is depressed that she's losing Den for good. When Den says he wants a divorce, she lies that she has only six months to live.

NOVEMBER

Den says he'll drop the divorce idea and takes 'sick' Angie to Italy. In Venice, Den spots Jan with Dario, her old flame, and manages to meet her. Kelvin, encouraged by Colin, applies for sponsorship to attend college. The Fowlers return from the pub one night and find they've been robbed. Pauline realises that Arthur was the 'burglar' – he'd hoped to cover up the fact that he spent the Club money. He's soon arrested and confesses. Pauline hears that Mark is in a detention centre for burglary and assault. There is good news – Michelle has married Lofty in a register office. The Walford 'Ripper' is at work –

two attacks on women are reported. Coming home on the Orient Express, tipsy Angie tells a barman about her lie and Den overhears.

Barry moves in with Colin.

DECEMBER

Tony and Hannah are unhappy about Kelvin's affair with an older woman, Carmel. Young Barry moves in with Colin. Lofty and Michelle have a short honeymoon, paid for by Lofty's Aunt Irene. Arthur is morose, childlike and snappy with Pete. Pauline makes him apologise. Pat advises Mary on fleecing men. Charlie is back and stealing from Dot again. Brewery manager James Willmott-Brown finally buys Debs' house. At a big gathering for Christmas dinner at The Vic, Den gives Angie the surprise he has promised – her divorce papers. Babysitting Martin and Vicki that night, Arthur breaks down and wrecks the living room.

JANUARY

Pauline knows that Arthur, who is so distracted that he doesn't feel anything when hot tea is spilled on his lap, must go to hospital. Naima gives her cousin Rezaul, who is sent by her family to 'sort out' the shop, a chilly reception. The local attacker stalks Sharon but Den rescues her. Mary, still picking up men in The Vic, is beaten up but tells Sue that 'professional' girls did it to warn her off. Later she tells social worker Carmel that a client struck her. Dot reluctantly sees Dr Legg's new partner, Dr Singh, who prescribes hormone treatment for her menopausal problems. Kelvin celebrates turning eighteen with a noisy party and a stripagram. Mehmet swindles Kathy and Michelle out of the money for a large batch of jumpers.

FEBRUARY

Den, Pete and Tony give Mehmet a beating. Pat, Sue and Carmel warn Mary that Annie might be taken into care. She leaves the child alone again, but luckily Ethel and Dot step in. Willmott-Brown leaves the brewery to run The Dagmar.

Arthur's distracted and at his wits end with worry.

With Angie and Sharon away, Jan offers to help at The Vic and proves to be a disaster. She tries to fire Pat and does sack Pauline. Barry and Nick Cotton smash into

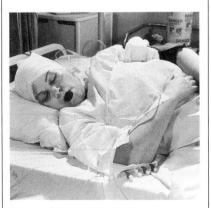

Pat lies in intensive care.

Ali's car; Colin makes Barry report it to the police. The 'Ripper' viciously attacks Pat, leaving her unconscious in the gardens. Wicksy and Pete are suspects and Pete angrily hits a policeman.

MARCH

Another woman is attacked and again Pete has no alibi. Colin is frantic when he discovers his Filofax is missing; Barry has hidden it as a joke. Kathy starts training for the Samaritans. Willmott-Brown says 'yes' when Angie asks for the job of manageress at The Dagmar. Sharon is becoming keen on Wicksy. Ian is keen on Tina. Arthur, home for a break from hospital, angers Pauline by confiding in Mary. Sue finds a lump in her breast and Debs insists she goes to the clinic. Tests there show it's harmless. When Dot sees Barry and Colin's single set of sheets in the launderette, she concludes, to her horror, that they are gay!

APRIL

Den and Jan argue. She leaves, saying she'll marry Dario. Kathy refuses a request to meet her illegitimate daughter. When the 'Ripper' attacks Debs in the launderette, Pete catches him. Det. Sgt Terry Rich takes statements and later asks Debs out. Soon they're engaged. Sharon and Wicksy go away for a 'dirty' weekend which turns out to be very clean, although Angie and Den don't believe it; they're furious. Angie wants half of everything that Den owns. This turns out to be debts, some of which are owed to Sparrow, the new man at the brewery. Mary again leaves Annie, who throws a cot blanket over the electric fire and starts a blaze.

Den and his new love, Mags.

MAY

Mags Czajkowski gives Den catering advice and soon they're having an affair. At his trial, Arthur is sentenced to twenty-eight days in prison for theft. Pauline and Michelle start to pay people the money they lost through the Christmas Club. Pete is fined two hundred pounds for hitting the policeman. Mary's mother arrives and takes Annie back to Stockport. Dot and Ethel, who have been living together, are to swap council homes with Tom. Then Ethel asks Pat to move out from Dr Legg's so she can have her old room back. Michelle refuses to

accept Den's money for Vicki's first birthday present. Pauline eavesdrops and it confirms her theory that Den is Vicki's father. Tony tells Kelvin he's returning to Trinidad.

JUNE

Angie is shamed into admitting her heavy drinking after Sharon video-tapes her at The Dagmar. A

No more drinking for Angie?

video juke box that Den hires attracts drugs pushers. Police nab the son of a member of The Firm, the local mafia ring, for drug dealing, but The Firm force Den to frame an innocent boy instead. Barry worries that his summer flu is really the first symptom of Aids. He tells his brother Graham that he's gay, but it comes as

1987

Mary Smith and her new friend Rod Norman.

no surprise. Arthur, now out of prison, begins work at The Dagmar but his first wage packet is stolen; Sue has a whip-round for him. Tom and Arthur, each tending pub window-boxes for London In Bloom, are again in competition. The Dagmar wins second prize. Ian and Tina set up home together.

JULY

Den throws out an umbrella, which is one that Tom gave Dot. It costs him forty-three pounds in taxi fares for Ethel to replace it. Naima's family sends another cousin, Farrukh, and she expects to dislike him but doesn't. Angie and Sharon move into the flat above The Dagmar. Wicksy, tired of

Sharon, fancies Mags. Brad tells Den he must travel to Morocco as a courier for The Firm. The Vic's and The Dagmar's football teams prepare for an 'unfriendly'. Sue and Ali learn they may be evicted by Saeed's cousin, Ashraf Karim, because the flat is to be sold. Ali gambles the café's takings to raise the deposit but loses the money. Carmel moves into one of the Carpenters' flats, helped by her brother Darren and hampered by his son Junior.

AUGUST

Den sacks Wicksy for chatting up Mags. Luckily there's a job for him at The Dagmar. Mags drops Den and moves into Kelvin's flat. Kelvin's good A level

results mean he'll soon be off to university. Lofty talks to Michelle about their having a baby. Michelle confides to Den that she's already bored with Lofty and offers to go away with him. Mary's new friend Rod offers to clean her flat so it will be suitable for Annie's return. The Vic football team win only after Den insists they play dirty; Colin and Mags are shocked. On the other hand, The Vic Ladies' Darts Team wins their match in a fair fight. Donna Ludlow, the secret daughter of Kathy, arrives.

SEPTEMBER

On the Darts Team's outing to Greenwich, Pauline meets Derek Taylor, who takes a shine to her and later turns up in The Vic. Pat meets her old flame, Frank Butcher, who proposes marriage. Den gives Donna a job at The Vic, but when Pete questions her about her past, he's puzzled. Dr Legg hires Darren to paint the surgery. Darren sub-contracts Rod but Carmel ends up paying a proper painter to do it. Tina's parents find out she's living with Ian and take her home. Dot, who has recently been stung on the bottom by a bee, is a success at organising Ozcabs. Lofty

44

excitedly thinks Michelle is pregnant; she's relieved to find she isn't. Sharon gets Den and Angie together and they end up in bed.

OCTOBER

Mary is upset when her parents arrive without Annie. Willmott-Brown is grumpily cleaning off the anti-yuppy graffiti that has been daubed on his house and The Dagmar. On her

Willmott-Brown in The Dagmar.

eighteenth birthday, Sharon goes to church and meets a nice young man, Duncan, the curate. Barry takes Donna to a disco. Arthur borrows money to take Pauline on the town and spend the night in a hotel.

Sue tells Ali she's pregnant, and there's no mistake this time. Wicksy is living with Mags but she's having no luck in buying a place of her own. Ethel foresees a dark man in Dot's life. Sadly there are two – Charlie and Nick, who meet for the first time.

NOVEMBER

Angie, tiring of The Dagmar, returns to The Vic where womanless Den invites her away for the weekend. Cheered by this, she plots to use Darren to make Den jealous. Darren won't play ball and Den finds out. Colin, having trouble with his design work, also has problems with jury service. Den, on Brad's orders, tries to blackmail him to acquit the defendant in a gangland trial; he refuses. Ethel has another fall and Dr Legg talks to her about sheltered housing. Charlie sells Ian cheap salmon for The Vic's Bonfire Night snacks; food poisoning strikes all round. Mary's father brings Annie back.

DECEMBER

Darren is stashing porn videos in Carmel's flat. Colin's flat is burgled but the police are more interested in

his gay relationship than the crime. Rezaul catches Charlie shop-lifting. Both he and Dot appear in court on the same day. After it's reported in the *Gazette*, Dot's agony is made worse because she's sacked from the launderette

Sharon wants to marry Duncan.

for it. Sharon asks Duncan if they can get engaged. The Dagmar yuppies finally wear Angie down. She storms out and goes back to The Vic. Den and she agree to become business partners there. Colin, realising it's over with Barry, sends him home to confront his father. On Christmas Eve, Mary's father kidnaps Annie and crashes his car while drunk. Thankfully the child is unharmed. Michelle tells Pauline she's pregnant.

JANUARY

Angie Watts is rushed to hospital, seriously ill with kidney failure. Lofty's joy at Michelle's pregnancy soon changes to despair when she has an abortion, paid for by Den. He calls her a murderer, and throws her belongings out of their flat. Later Pauline confronts Den, who admits he is Vicki's father. It's a month of comings and goings: the Karim family take over the

The Karims move into the foodstore in the Square.

foodstore; Ethel moves into sheltered housing; Barry leaves Colin; Frank Butcher visits Pat, his old flame; Kenny Beale, older brother of Pauline and Pete, is due home from New Zealand.

Pat Wicks has some humiliating news for Pete and Kenny Beale.

FEBRUARY

Kenny Beale arrives with his daughter, Elizabeth, to a series of rows over Simon Wicks' parentage. Pat Wicks, urged by Lou to come clean, will only tell Pete and Kenny that they were both useless in bed. Den wonders if he was mentioned too. Barry and Ian become partners in running a disco at the Community Centre, using equipment hired through Darren. Sue is panicking about her unborn child's health and Carmel has to reassure her. Kathy learns that Donna has been ringing her at the Samaritans.

MARCH

On his eighteenth birthday, Ian kisses Elizabeth. Den finally runs out of excuses for not visiting Angie in hospital. They talk about starting again in a new pub, but first she takes a holiday in Spain. Frank and Pat ask about taking over The Vic. Dot, searching for Tom, takes a peep at Darren's 'Cultural Night' at the Community Centre. She faints at finding it's a porn video show and a strip-tease act. Mags drives out of Albert Square, disillusioned. Kathy is asked to leave the Samaritans but is offered work at The Dagmar. Sue goes into labour, with Lofty and Pauline acting as midwives; baby Ali is born.

APRIL

Donna, flirting with Ian but keener on Wicksy, reveals to Kathy that she is her daughter. Kathy can't feel pleased. Angie reveals that she had an affair with a man called Sonny in Spain. Sue finds that their neighbour, Alan McIntyre,

Time's up for Tom Clements.

has bought their flat. Den is 'hired' to work for The Firm. Lofty leaves the Square to become a handyman in a children's home; only Den, out walking Roly, sees him go. Tom, collecting glasses at The Vic, collapses in the gents and dies. Dr Legg's new partner, his nephew Dr David Samuels, examines Colin, who is increasingly concerned about his health.

MAY

Ian is disgusted when Kathy tells him that Donna is her daughter. To Pete's alarm, he moves in with Barry, who is living in Ethel's old flat. Willmott-Brown, smitten with Kathy, buys her expensive scent while Pete's jealousy mounts. Michelle and Sharon throw a party in the new flat Den has bought from McIntyre. Angie upsets Sharon with the news that she is off to live with Sonny in Marbella. Mary, depressed and on speed, scoops up Annie and a few belongings and takes a bus out of Walford.

JUNE

Darren offers his protection services to both Willmott-Brown and Brad, who has him beaten

up. Pauline tells Michelle to forget Den. Den tries it on with Joanne, the manager of the wine bar. Later she puts him down firmly. Frank and

Den and Joanne put on the ritz.

Pat become landlords of The Queen Vic but Pat begins to feel the strain of living with Frank's kids. Kathy is pushed to tell Donna that she's the product of a rape – news which Donna passes on to Wicksy in the hope of luring him away from his new girl-friend, Cindy Williams. To Ian's fury, the disco equipment he bought from Darren is repossessed by a finance company. Darren then disappears.

JULY

While Pete is busy driving Lou to Leigh-on-Sea, Willmott-Brown pressures Kathy to stay late at his flat. Then he rapes her. Den finds her crying in a corner. Soon The Dagmar is in flames, as Den watches the results of his handiwork. The police are called and Willmott-Brown is charged with rape. He claims Kathy consented. Arthur is sacked by the Karims. Cindy and Wicksy spend a night together. Barry leaves Walford to work as a DJ in a disco. Lou summons the family and distributes advice and 'treasures'. That night she dies in her sleep. Later Pete toasts 'that bloody old bag' in The Vic.

AUGUST

Ethel and Benny Bloom are courting. Dot tries to stop smoking. However, the strain of hosting Sunday lunch for the Fowlers, and Charlie's theft of her holiday money, drive her into lighting up again. Ian passes his catering exams then starts work in Ali's café. Frank takes Wicksy on as a barman but Donna is sacked after a brawl with Cindy. Den is asked by The Firm to take

Saying goodbye to Lou.

the rap and go to jail for The Dagmar fire, so he decides to go on the run. He leaves money and 'insurance' statements with Pat. Joanne blackmails Rod into tipping off the police that Den is leaving.

SEPTEMBER

Frank's battleaxe of a mother, Mo Butcher, blusters in and clashes with Pat. Ricky Butcher is chatting up Shireen Karim. Donna, turfed out of Sharon's flat and Rod, turfed out of Mary's, move into a squat together. Sharon tells Duncan their engagement is off. Carmel agrees to allow her white boyfriend, Matthew, to move into her flat. Dr Legg and David disagree over whether or not to tell Colin that he has multiple sclerosis. At the magistrates' court, Pete lunges at Willmott-Brown.

The Dagmar goes up in flames. All Den's doing?

Den, dodging The Firm, gives himself up to the Manchester police and is sent to join Queenie, Barnsey and other grisly inmates of Dickens Hill Prison. Pat visits him there.

OCTOBER

Dot takes over the Square's Neighbourhood Watch scheme. Colin meets Guido Smith at the

Matthew and Carmel have to look after Aisha and Junior yet again.

wine bar. Cindy, upset at spotting Wicksy with another girl, busies herself in helping Ian with catering jobs. At Pauline's, where the two boys are lodging, they fight over Cindy. Michelle, working at Dr Legg's surgery, becomes close to David. Pauline despairs as her home is turned into a tip

by Ian and Wicksy. Ricky makes an unsuccessful play for Shireen when she babysits Vicki. Den is suspected of 'grassing' in jail.

NOVEMBER

Kathy and Pete return from a holiday and she tells him she won't sleep with him any more. In Pat's absence, Mo causes havoc by rearranging things at The Vic. Ricky is paid to tidy up for Ian and Wicksy at the Fowlers' until Arthur finds out. Sohail Karim is keen on Diane Butcher but she isn't interested. Den is beaten up in his cell and Sharon winces at the sight of his bruises when she visits him. Pat informs Joanne that Den has not told the police about The Firm. Vic, a fellow prisoner, is tested for Aids. Rod rails at Donna for taking heroin; she shrugs it off. Carmel and Matthew decide to get married.

DECEMBER

Ian drops Donna as a waitress when Rod tells him of her addiction. Ali and Mehmet, trying to run Ozcabs together, run up gambling debts in the wine bar. Ian loans them some money. Guido moves in with Colin. Shireen's father, angry at her having been alone with Ricky, asks Dr Legg to check that she's still a virgin but he refuses. Pete is caught and charged with drinking and driving. Donna invites Ali to the squat for sex, only to blackmail him later. Ian and Michelle plan to work on Christmas Day, which wrecks the family celebrations. Nick Cotton moves into Den's cell and confesses that he was the one who killed Reg Cox.

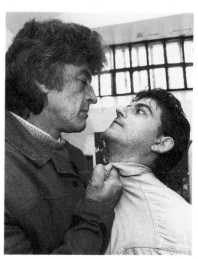
Barnsey teaches Nick a lesson.

1988

49

JANUARY

Kathy tricks Willmott-Brown when he tries to bribe her to drop the rape charges and the police catch him. In jail Den learns that Queenie is tipping off the police about The Firm. The Queen Vic regulars hold a sit-in in favour of all-day opening. The Health Inspector examines the pub kitchen and orders a re-fit; reluctantly, Pat uses some of Den's money to pay for it. Dr Legg has to tell Colin he has multiple sclerosis. Kathy explains to a miserable Pete that their marriage is over. Shireen runs away from her boarding school. Carmel and Matthew marry but he is not pleased when his mother attends the wedding.

Den *en route* for the trial.

FEBRUARY

Pete, drinking heavily, crashes Mehmet's car and is arrested. Ian and Cindy get engaged. On the way to his trial, Den is seized by Brad but later escapes. Colin leaves Guido and his friends in the Square and goes to live with a brother in Bristol. Den arranges to meet Michelle by the canal but Mantel from The Firm has her followed. As Den walks away from their brief meeting a shot is fired by a man holding a bunch of daffodils. There's the sound of a splash. It seems Den has fallen into the water.

MARCH

Frank opens a car lot on the Portakabin site and sells Ian a jeep. Tension builds up for Carmel and Matthew when her father has a stroke and she is pressed to take Darren's children, Junior and Aisha, full time. Matthew's violent temper begins to show. Donna, now living with Dot, spreads a rumour that Colin has Aids. She then tells Sue she has slept with Ali. He, jealous at seeing Sue with Mehmet, fights with his brother then throws Sue out of their flat. Dot hears that she has a grand-daughter. The police tell Sharon and Michelle that they believe Den is dead.

APRIL

Michelle tells Sharon that Den is Vicki's father. Instead of being comforted, Sharon is angry and confused. Later she tries to give Michelle Den's money. Arthur also learns the truth about Den. Depressed and sick, Donna dies in Dot's living room after choking on her own

Kathy takes the stand.

vomit. David criticises Dr Legg's handling of her heroin addiction; Kathy blames herself. Pat decides to let a room and builder Paul Priestley takes it. Ian buys into Ali's business. Wicksy and Sharon become close again. At the gruelling rape trial, Willmott-Brown is found guilty and jailed for three years.

MAY

Mo helps her old pal Marge Green, who was Brown Owl until young Melody, Junior's friend, joined and turned Walford Brownies into a pack of tiny lager-louts. Pat is forced to give a car to her husband, Brian Wicks, before he will finalise their divorce; she tells Frank it's for her Auntie Mabel. Cindy has her wicked way with Wicksy in the pub. Vicki falls victim to meningitis but pulls through in hospital. Matthew beats Carmel viciously after she teases him. Ali finds Sue at Hassan's grave and snatches their baby, Ali. Tragically deranged, Sue is taken to hospital.

Arthur playing *Cat and Mouse*.

JUNE

Lively Northern lass Julie Cooper arrives in the Square, as does Trevor Short. He's looking for work and his pal Paul. Arthur wins the star prize, a holiday, on a TV quiz, *Cat and Mouse*. Cindy, living with Ian in a tower block flat, discovers she is pregnant. Dot is delighted to meet Hazel, who has turned up out of the blue and has a baby. She claims it is Nick's, and called Dorothy Nicola in Dot's honour. Charlie discovers the baby is Hazel's sister's child and Hazel has been using her to get money from Dot. Ian takes over the café. Pat and Frank marry in grand style and Mo surprises them with a street party. Dot discovers that Charlie is a bigamist when she meets his other wife, Joan Leggett.

JULY

Frank's six-year-old daughter Janine comes to live at the pub and turns out to be prone to throwing tantrums. Pauline, fearing she may need a serious gynaecological operation, cancels her hospital appointments and tries hypnotherapy instead. Julie and Diane are rivals for Paul, who is now busily working with Trevor to convert the fish and chip shop into Julie's hairdressing salon. Matthew is enraged to learn that Carmel shared a working lunch with David. In a struggle with a knife, Matthew is badly injured by Junior. Unpaid-for equipment in the café is

Hazel tells Dot she's a grandmother at last – but is she?

So happy together – Michelle and her new love, Danny.

repossessed. Ali, sacked as Frank's car salesman and driving a minicab again, is forced to leave baby Ali with unregistered child-minders. A jubilant Pete wins one thousand pounds on the premium bonds.

AUGUST

Pete leaves for a trip to New Zealand. Michelle takes Danny Whiting, a new friend, to dinner with Sharon and Wicksy at the pizza bar. Michelle knows he is married with three children and tries to stop seeing him. She also finds out that Cindy is trying to rekindle Wicksy's interest. Ruth, David's girlfriend from Israel, arrives. Janine takes Pat's ring and hides it in a plant pot. When Trevor comes across it, Frank accuses him of stealing it. Michelle accepts Julie's offer of work at the salon. Janine runs away from home.

SEPTEMBER

After two days Frank finds Janine in a Dormobile on his car lot. Ricky chats up Julie's apprentice, Marie. Julie chats up the new stall-holder, Laurie Bates, but he

Runaway Janine Butcher.

is also interested in meeting Kathy. Hazel arrives at Dot's, having been beaten up by Nick. Dot forgives her and takes her in. Arthur and Pauline go on holiday, their prize from the quiz, to Minorca. Abroad for the first time! Mo runs the fruit and veg stall meanwhile. Benny Bloom has died and Ethel discovers she is to inherit two thousand pounds in his will. For a while Benny's daughter threatens to contest it. Wicksy and Sharon, now living together and also working in The Vic, can barely control yobs in the pub. Ricky, showing off to Marie, zooms around in a Mini and knocks down Pauline, who is taken to hospital.

OCTOBER

While Ian is pushing Cindy to agree to a wedding date, she tells Wicksy that the baby is his; he seems unaffected. Julie wins The Vic talent contest with a dirty song. Ali loses at cards with McIntyre, who throws him and his furniture out of the flat. Cindy's wedding to Ian is a disastrous round of rows with Pete and Ian. They storm off, leaving her sobbing. The Butchers take over Doris' bed and

Cindy and Ian in happier times.

breakfast business. Trevor, living at Mo's, hears worrying noises; the culprit is a pigeon. Michelle is unable to split from Danny. Junior and Melody pelt Dot with eggs on Hallowe'en.

NOVEMBER

Laurie tells Kathy that he's serious about her. Pete argues with him. The DHSS man catches up with Trevor, who has been claiming the dole while working as a painter and decorator, but eventually he decides not to prosecute. Ashraf Karim is discovered to have a mistress, Stella. His wife, Sufia, is distraught. Hazel fails to get Rod interested in her. Marge, coping with her sick old mum, gives up her work at the launderette. Danny, who is staying with Michelle,

witnesses Marge being mugged and retrieves her handbag for her, but he won't give his name to the police. Dot is disturbed by the sight of a rat in the rubbish and begins an anti-litter campaign.

DECEMBER

When Marge's mother has a second stroke and is taken into hospital, Ethel suggests that she, Reggie (Ethel's dancing partner and pal from the sheltered housing), Marge, Mo and Dot take a holiday in Clacton. Once there, Marge meets Mr Conroy and romance is in the air. He proposes, but she rejects him because of her mother. When the news is phoned through of the old woman's death, Conroy has already packed up and left. Pauline spends Christmas in hospital after having a hysterectomy. Michelle and Danny celebrate early and he clumsily gives her his wife's Christmas card. Paul returns to Leeds without saying goodbye to heart-broken Diane. Arthur organises a treasure hunt. And Cindy, on Boxing Day, gives birth to a boy. Later, left alone with Wicksy, she reminds him that the child is his.

Marie, Julie and Michelle man the phones in Julie's Salon.

JANUARY

Miserable, Diane Butcher runs away from home because she believes her family forgot her birthday. In fact, they'd prepared a surprise party for her. A shaken Frank rushes off to Leeds believing she may have followed Paul there. A girl's body is then found but it's not Diane's. Days later, Frank misses her phone call. Two-timing Danny tells Michelle that she must move with him to Newcastle or it's all over between them. Meanwhile, his wife, Mandy, tracks him down. Pete's friend Barbara from New Zealand visits Pauline and is welcomed in. Michelle overhears Wicksy tell Cindy that he wants her and baby Steven. Sufia Karim packs her belongings but Ashraf tells her his affair with Stella is over. It seems it is, thanks to Stella calling it off.

FEBRUARY

Marge bids goodbye to Albert Square with brave smiles but Mo knows that looking after cousin Fred's mum on a cruise isn't going to be much fun. Pat wants Frank's troublesome daughter Janine to see a psychologist, but Frank is

Diane decides to return home.

appalled. Eventually they go to family therapy, with some success. Michelle is about to go North with Danny but changes her mind. Later Mandy confirms that Danny lied about who left whom. The Mitchell brothers swagger into The Vic. They've set up a motor repair business under the railway arches. On an impulse, Rod leaves with Hazel and her friend for India. Paul arrives to tell Frank he hasn't seen Diane, then he leaves for Leeds again with Trevor.

MARCH

Dot Cotton wins ten thousand pounds at bingo, but no sooner has she met the Mayor and been presented with the cheque

than her son Nick Cotton gets off the bus in Walford. He tells his mother that he's a born-again Christian. Kathy ends a half-hearted affair with Laurie Bates. Julie's business has floundered and the Mitchells are hustling for her lease, at a cheap price. Cindy and Ian move into Colin's flat, helped by Wicksy. Pete buys his sister's share of the stall. A scruffy Diane, tired of street-life, phones Frank and asks him to meet her at Kings Cross. He brings her home. Taylor, a middle-aged photographer for whom she modelled, follows.

The canal is dredged for Den's body.

APRIL

Nick helps Frank remove a nude statue of Diane that has been left in the Square. Frank, believing that Diane was a prostitute when living rough, smashes it angrily. When Taylor gives a college lecture, Frank confronts him, making things worse with Diane. Nick puts Dot on a dubious diet to 'cure her migraines'; she begins to feel unwell.

A marriage is arranged.

Shireen meets the likeable Jabbar, the boy it's arranged she'll marry, but meanwhile her father picks up his affair with Stella again. What seems to be Den's body is fished out of the canal. Sharon, deeply upset, disappears. Michelle has to arrange the funeral.

The Fowlers at Den's funeral.

MAY

Den's prison mates turn the funeral into a rowdy party. Sharon has returned in time for it but is now intent on tracing her real parents. Frank and Pat decide they can't run the B & B, car lot and The Vic, so Sharon and Wicksy plan to apply for the pub tenancy. Wicksy's gift of an expensive dress at a party for Cindy's birthday makes Sharon guess what's behind Wicksy's coolness to her – his feelings for Cindy. Pauline quietly gets a job at the paint factory. Pete leads the other traders to oppose the council's scheme to clear the market. Ethel, certain that Nick is poisoning Dot, asks Charlie Cotton to look for the poison. He finds some and the police are called, but Dot revives and sends them off.

JUNE

Jabbar's uncle spots Ashraf in a restaurant with Stella and calls off his nephew's engagement to Shireen. The Karims move to Bristol. All may not be lost, if Sufia and the women of Jabbar's family succeed. Nick's noxious shepherd's pie is whisked away from Dot but Grant Mitchell ends up eating it. She changes her will, Nick feels guilty (or caught out) and stops her eating a 'special' meal, then leaves. Kendle, Michelle's boss at the council, tries to bribe Pete through Ian to stop protesting about the closure of the market. Kathy overhears Cindy begging Wicksy to stay in Walford and realises what's going on between them.

JULY

The Vic's new landlord, Eddie Royle, arrives. Sharon tracks down the address of Carol, her mother. When she telephones, Carol

55

is in hospital. Flustered, Sharon rushes there and finds she has had a baby. Carol's husband, Ron, makes Sharon unwelcome. The Taverniers, Dot's new West Indian neighbours, have

The Taverniers move in.

their house blessed. As the council's plan to end the market proceeds, Kathy and Michelle plot to expose Kendle as corrupt. The Butchers go on holiday to the Isle of Wight. In their absence, Diane paints a giant mural on the side of the house and Ricky meets Sam, the Mitchells' perky young sister. Wicksy and Cindy spend a day together.

AUGUST

Mo Butcher forgets to turn off her bath taps and causes a flood. Sharon warns Wicksy to tell Ian before she does that he's not Steven's father. Cindy finally tells Ian the truth. He reacts by madly driving off, crashing, breaking bones and ending up in Intensive Care. He seems to remember nothing when he regains consciousness. Hattie Tavernier admits that she helped her twin Lloyd with his schoolwork and that her own suffered as a result. Eddie stops Pete buying an illegal driving licence from Grant. Sam teases Ricky by sleeping in his bed and making him take her and her friend Jamie to the zoo. The increasingly forgetful Mo undergoes tests. Cindy goes to her parents' house in Devon where Wicksy joins her. Out of the blue, Mark Fowler writes to Michelle.

SEPTEMBER

A consultant confirms that Mo is suffering from dementia. Michelle persuades Diane to return to school. Arthur is delivering 'packages' for Grant and his brother Phil. Ian, discharged from hospital, is urged by Pete to travel to Devon to save his marriage. He's horrified to see Wicksy there with Cindy. Later, he hurls a brick and his crutch through a window at them, but Wicksy invites him in to talk. He passes out, tired and

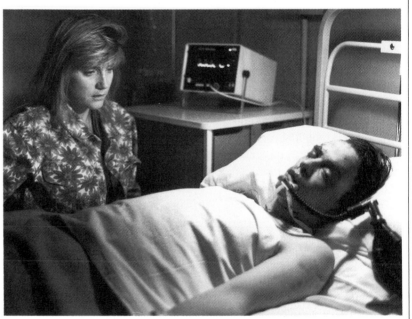

Ian lies unconscious in intensive care after the smash.

drunk. Next morning he takes Cindy's father's shotgun and goes home, where he bags up Cindy's belongings. When Wicksy and Cindy return, Pete has declared cold war in the Square. Mark arrives, much to his parents' delight.

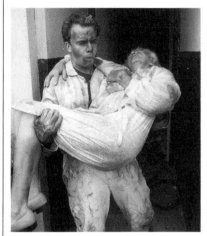

Mark saves Mo from the fire.

OCTOBER

Ian seeks a blood test to prove who's Steven's father. Kathy asks Eddie to sack Wicksy, but he responds by asking her out. Dithering Mo sets fire to her house. Mark is arrested when helping Arthur by delivering the Mitchell's suspect car log-books. The Beale family go out for a meal but the Butchers arrive at the same restaurant. They argue loudly and have to leave. Pete lets Kathy know he still cares but

she tells him not to hope. Sharon and Carol continue their uneasy meetings. Eddie's dad, John, and Jules Tavernier plan to play poker games in Dot's house.

NOVEMBER

Jules wins at poker for John but is paid in chickens which Mo takes to the B & B. Michelle persuades Phil Mitchell to go to the police over Mark's arrest. Phil suggests a gardening business for Arthur. Eddie is grilled by detectives over police corruption and meets several former police colleagues and his old boss, Penton. He proves the man is corrupt, forcing him to resign. Money seems to be missing from The Vic's till. Is the

Eddie and the long arm of the law.

culprit the new barman Clyde Tavernier or a hard-up Wicksy? Grant wants to buy Sharon's flat, but at a reduced price. Mark and Diane become friends. Busy with his catering business, Ian persuades Kathy to run the café for him.

DECEMBER

Young Jason is stealing from Pete's stall, but unsuspecting Pete believes he is a lonely child and lets him help. Celestine Tavernier, who works in the dole office, has to warn Arthur that he must sign off. Clyde goes to Bristol to see his son, Kofi, and his late girlfriend's parents tell him that they plan to emigrate to Jamaica, taking the child with them. Diane and Mark bump into Disa, heavily pregnant, in London. Ian is discovered to be behind The Vic's lost money; it was a plot to incriminate Wicksy. Ian offers him extra work at evening functions. As Christmas arrives, Ian seems to have a death wish because he drives himself and Wicksy in a van with faulty brakes. They crash and have a fight. Wicksy and Cindy decide they must leave Walford. A baby in a cardboard box is left at Diane's door.

JANUARY

To Diane's relief, Disa begins to feel love for her baby. But when a stranger called Ken asks Dot to pass twenty pounds on to Disa, she is mystified. Pete is worried about cheeky young Jason, who seems to prefer helping at the fruit stall to going home. When the boy stays at Pete's flat, he is threatened by the boy's father. Pete learns that Jason

Dot's the heroine of the hour.

has been beaten and, at Kathy's bidding, informs the Social Services. Ian's waitresses walk out on him and Sharon decides she won't work for him because

he's so exploitative. Kathy is not pleased to spot Eibhlin kissing Eddie, but she's furious when he rings her at the Samaritans to explain. The Vic team lose at snooker to The Rose and Crown. Mark confesses to a shocked but concerned Diane that he is HIV positive. Ken kidnaps Disa's baby.

FEBRUARY

Dot tricks Ken into a showdown and rescues the baby. Fowler and Son win the contract to look after the Square's gardens. Etta needs to attend a teaching course but it clashes with a Paris holiday that Celestine has planned. Mark is the dark stranger seen in the tea leaves who dances with Ethel on her seventy-fifth birthday, which has been forgotten by the others. Phil Mitchell attends court, flanked by Arthur in a suit, to answer the charge of stealing car log books. Diane returns from a school trip to France, although she has no fun at Ricky's eighteenth birthday party. Moody Mark doesn't attend: he's chatting up Lorna at a disco. Before they leave for Sunderland, Sandra, Disa's mum, confronts Ken in jail about abusing her daughters.

MARCH

Etta applies for the head teacher's job, and asks to be sterilised only to discover she is pregnant. A car with a bootful of banknotes is left in the Mitchells' garage. Menacing heavies later turn up and wreck the Mitchell's flats, demanding it back. Dot, worried about a lump

Trouble for the Taverniers.

on her chest, is alarmed when Dr Legg asks her to undress after Ethel's joke that he's 'interested' in her. The lump turns out to be a boil. Newcomer Rachel Kominsky rejects Michelle as a lodger when she hears about Vicki. But Michelle does get a new job, selling time share flats. Mark can't respond at Aids counselling. He cheers up after he persuades Pauline to give him five hundred pounds towards a car – then uses it as a deposit on a new, powerful motor bike. Pauline learns she's lost her paint factory job. Ian plants a stolen computer at The Dagmar so that Jackie Stone, who is squatting there, will be evicted.

APRIL

Arthur spots a valuable stamp from the villain's car on Sharon's letter to her bank. Despite a frantic chase it's posted and ends up on *Blue Peter*. Eddie flirts mildly with Sharon, which leads Grant to beat him so savagely that Eddie needs brain surgery. A despairing Grant tries to re-enlist in the army, while Frank tries and fails to round up a posse of residents to help 'teach him a lesson'. Meanwhile, Eibhlin visits from Ireland and Eddie proposes to her. The

Janine brings home head lice from her school.

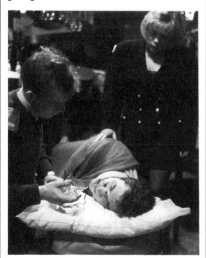

Eddie is badly beaten by Grant.

Mitchells' mother, Peggy, arrives to sort out both Grant and Sam, who is running away to sleep in the garage. Grant fails the psychiatric test for the army. A test shows that Etta's unborn child has sickle-cell anaemia like Lloyd and, despite Celestine's pleas and threats to leave, she has an abortion.

MAY

Sharon struggles to control a gang of loudmouths in The Vic when dispirited Eddie won't leave his room or call the police. Finally he's forced to eject them – but only with Grant's help. Martin and Janine bring their families presents from school – head lice. Ian offers to sell the café to his mother, then inflates the price by approaching Frank. Finally Kathy, Pauline and Frank

become partners at the old price. At the same time, Pat signs up for one of Michelle's time share flats. Rachel delights Michelle by shaming the time share company into paying Michelle the commission they owe her and then offering her the room Karen has left. Burglars ransack Pete's flat and he moves in temporarily with Ian. Ricky and Sam become engaged and arrange a family tea on her sixteenth birthday to announce it. Her outraged mother forbids them to meet . . . but they sneak off to an Ilford hotel to seal their union. The Mitchells tempt Clyde back to boxing. Mark's former girlfriend Gill visits.

JUNE

Mark denies he is HIV positive when Gill tells him that she is. Mark

Back again – Nick Cotton.

suggests marriage to Diane. At Rachel's house-warming party, Michelle feels socially out of her depth and has to turf Graham out of her bed. A tramp-like Nick Cotton, addicted to heroin, is found in Pete's lock-up garage. Pete is further sickened when Ian shrugs off the injuries suffered by one of the Dagmar renovation workmen and so moves in with Pauline. Den's former prison mate Johnny Harris tells Sharon that D. S. Manning, an old friend of Eddie's, is checking up on Grant's dodgy dealings. Sharon is able to remove incriminating packages from the garage in the nick of time. Sam and Ricky are caught canoodling outside her school gates and there's a fight in the street. But after Sam finishes her school exams, she dons a dark wig and Ricky whisks her away in supposed secrecy. The RAC route map to Gretna Green that he leaves behind gives a fairly strong clue to their destination, though.

JULY

Phil, Grant and Kevin hare up to Scotland after Ricky and Sam. Frank and Pat follow (after she has packed a nice outfit, just in case). Despite having to wait two weeks and camp in a field, the elopers marry, with Frank and Pat's knowledge and with Sam wearing a fellow run-away's dress.

Ricky and Sam make it official.

Meanwhile Grant buys a marriage licence and Sharon says 'yes', only to have Eddie sack her for it and then suggest a name change for the pub. Furious, Sharon decides to fight for The Vic herself. Dot seems unmoved by Nick's addiction. Soon she hears worse news: Charlie has been killed in a road accident. In her grief, Dot decides to help her son. The funeral is held on the same day as a grand church blessing for Sam and Ricky. Michelle celebrates her twenty-second birthday drunkenly, ending up in bed with Clyde. Mark recognises Joe Wallace, Ian's new chef, as a visitor to the Aids centre.

AUGUST

Michelle decides to return to college, thanks to Rachel's string-pulling. Clyde is ignoring Michelle but Rachel is pursuing Mark, who has split up with Diane, now working in France. His friendship with Joe makes Rachel wonder if Mark is gay, though. Arthur, Pete and Frank gang up to oppose The Vic's name-change. Waitressing for Ian in the holidays means late nights for Hattie, which angers her father. Her exam results are brilliant, though. Lloyd's are pretty good too but Sam's are awful. Clyde takes a thrashing in his second

1991

boxing bout until his opponent suddenly caves in. Sharon is alarmed to find the Mitchells have staked all their money on Clyde's next fight. She wins her unfair dismissal case but rages to find Eddie won't re-instate her. Eibhlin says she'll marry Eddie and move into The Vic. Dot, trying to reduce Nick's £80 a day heroin dependency, still needs to find a great deal of money and so persuades Pat to employ her again at the B & B. She also needs to 'score' for him. Nick steals and lies again. Jules and Ethel feel they must help Dot to be rid of him. Mark becomes Ian's driver.

SEPTEMBER

Vicki and Kofi start school but, much to her parents' dismay, Hattie wants to continue working for Ian. Diane phones from France to say she won't be returning yet. When Ian discovers Joe is HIV positive he sacks him. Rachel sleeps with Mark, then learns he is HIV positive. Eddie plans to rename the pub The Victoria Tavern. When the old name is taken down, Grant buys the letters for Sharon. Pete and Dot, who have imprisoned Nick in his

bedroom and forced him to go 'cold turkey', do not spot that he has a knife, is loosening the screws around bars on the windows and so can escape. Eddie's friend, a contact of Baker's, Clyde's forthcoming boxing opponent, tries to bribe Clyde to lose the fight.

Who murdered Eddie Royle?

Clyde is furious and argues with Eddie. Grant learns that Eddie tipped off the police about the Mitchell brothers' shady dealings and they curse him angrily and openly. Before having a nightcap with Eibhlin, Eddie takes Roly for a walk. Back inside, Nick looks out to see Eddie lying in the street, with Clyde standing over him

holding a knife. Soon Roly is barking and Dot, investigating, finds Eddie. He has been knifed in the heart. The police suspect both Grant, who has no sound alibi, and Clyde of murder. The Vic is closed.

OCTOBER

Sharon is granted a temporary licence and reopens The Vic. She and Grant decide to postpone their wedding, probably until the New Year. Pat returns behind the bar, a move which angers Frank, leaving Dot to manage the B & B. Michelle begins her degree course in English and Sociology at the Poly but receives no encouragement from her parents. Pauline is not pleased at Mark's flourishing affair with Rachel. Nick, now coping without drugs, smartens up his appearance, tells his mother he is a reformed character and searches for a job. He also tells the police he saw Clyde Tavernier holding a knife near Eddie's body. Before he can be arrested for the murder of Eddie Royle, Clyde goes on the run. 'Wanted' posters for Clyde go up around Walford. The heart-broken Taverniers shun the Cottons.

Weddings down Walford way

The Butchers celebrated in East End style.

Down in Walford they don't seem to go a bundle on weddings. Perhaps they know too well (unlike softer soap folk) that a box of confetti doesn't solve that many problems. Since 1985 there have been only a few weddings to which we, the guests at home, have been invited, three of them in 1989, and only one where it seemed worth our raising a glass. That was Pat and Frank's big day in June, a jolly street party for all of Albert Square, a knees-up with jellied eels to follow, organised with skill by Mo. It was hard luck on the cast, though. When the event was recorded six weeks earlier, the sun shone but there was also a Force Nine gale blowing and most of the actresses had to wear thermal vests under their thin fancy frocks. Luckily it was worth it: the couple's happiness seems to be lasting. But then they were each other's first true loves!

We haven't been invited to the register office dos. Debs married Terry Rich off-screen, and when Angie married an American early in 1991, we didn't even learn the chap's name. Also, though I hardly dare point it out, there have been a larger number of divorces and splittings up than weddings in *EastEnders*. Angie and Den, Michelle and Lofty, Kathy and Pete, Carmel and Matthew, Cindy and Ian – each once-hopeful happy couple untied the knot with bitterness and regrets.

Left: Michelle got as far as the church but realised she couldn't go through with the wedding.
Above: An anxious Lofty waited and waited and waited.
Below: Married at last, and Lofty was a proud man.

Michelle and Lofty's splicing was one of the saddest sagas in soap history. Their first wedding, a traditional white affair, in September 1986 (for which Arthur took fifteen hundred pounds from the Square's Christmas Club funds, a crime which resulted in both his breakdown and imprisonment), never took place. Michelle put on the dress, Lofty waited at the church, the sausage rolls and sandwiches curled up on the plates, but Michelle couldn't walk up the aisle. Two months later they went quietly to a register office with only the Fowlers to see it happen. Sadly, by April 1988, Lofty was forced to leave both Michelle and Walford.

Left: Pat and Frank Butcher cut their cake outside The Vic.
Below: Doomed from the word go – Cindy and Ian Beale's blackly comic wedding.

Carmel married handsome Matthew in a register office in January 1989. Carmel should have left him there and asked for a refund: he was so angry she had secretly invited his mother, Lynne, that he shook his new bride minutes after the ceremony. He apologised but they skipped their reception and went straight to the airport to start their honeymoon. By March he was hitting her. By July the violence had become so serious that the marriage was as good as dead.

Cindy and Ian Beale's nuptials in October of that year became a black comedy. Cindy wasn't so much a blushing bride as a browned-off bride. Poker-faced, pregnant and in deep red, she clearly wished she could have called the whole thing off by the time the Beale clan gathered at the register office. She drove Pete to storm out when his enthusiasm so infuriated her that she had to hit him. And one by one the guests at the Beales' flat ducked the flying insults and departed as the party broke up, leaving Cindy alone with her bad mood.

When Sam and Ricky eloped to Gretna Green, Scotland (well, a version of it near Elstree, Hertfordshire) they were joined in comic matrimony as Sam's burly brothers raced to prevent it. Later, when Frank Butcher insisted on a flash Walford church blessing, the event clashed with Charlie Cotton's funeral. Oh, well, this was *EastEnders* – no one expected uninterrupted merriment.

EastEnders was the first popular drama in which it was realised that the biggest stars were often the smallest. Babies not only made viewers 'Ooh!' and 'Aah!' but they made the whole story of Albert Square seem true to life. These weren't planned or pampered babies, but infants with all the usual illnesses, plus hard-pressed, hard-up young parents discovering that life is never the same once a child is born.

But all producers and actors know they have their work cut out when there are babies who might become upset at any moment on the set. Producers Corinne Hollingworth and Pat Sandys advertise locally for babies to ensure that the children and their mothers do not have to travel far to the Elstree Studios. They also try to make sure that scenes are rehearsed with dolls, so the babies are subjected to the shortest times possible on the set.

Even then, because of the strict laws controlling how long children can work, sometimes a child 'runs out of hours' and a doll or an understudy has to be used instead.

This happened with little Edward, the gorgeous beefy little boy who played Cindy's son Steven. (Ironically, the character was born two months prematurely and so was supposed to be small – but Edward was soon nicknamed 'Chunky' by Adam Woodyatt, who played his

Baby Faces

dad, Ian Beale.) Towards the end of his first year, Steven was one of the characters at the Square's Bonfire Night party with his mum. Michelle Collins, who played Cindy, revealed however that there was an impostor in his bootees.

'We had to use another baby for those scenes. Not only was she a girl, she also had bright red hair whereas Edward was fair. I had to keep pushing her hair back under her hat but lots of people still spotted it,' she recalled.

Sometimes the parents of the babies decide to move away and this means replacing a child. The parents of the first Vicki, Emma Henry, moved to Scotland and the search went on for a fair-haired girl to take over. Samantha Leigh Martin arrived in time to learn to call Sue Tully 'Mummy 'Shell' and, amusingly, to call Letitia Dean 'Daddy Sharon'. She has since become a real trooper, ad libbing with perfect timing in such scenes as the one where Den, newly out of prison, telephoned Michelle and Vicki picked up the phone. The scenes where she and her uncle, Pauline's little Martin, played by Jon Peyton Price, play together, chattering happily, have become favourites with viewers.

But viewers don't always get to hear the children's ad libbing. Wendy Richard recalled: 'I think it was when Pauline was away recuperating from her hysterectomy and I was off being a fairy in pantomime in Bromley, that there was a scene where Michelle came in and said to Arthur "Did you and Martin have a

Above: Jon Peyton Price who plays Martin.

proper supper?" and Arthur said "Yes, we had an Indian last night, didn't we, Martin?" Little Jon said "Yes, and we had a cowboy an' all." Another time we had to stop recording, I forget what it was we were talking about, but suddenly little Jon piped up with "I've been in an aeroplane to a far away place."

'It had to be edited out because there's no way Pauline's Martin could have been in an aeroplane going anywhere. Sometimes when he chimes in they leave it because it's so good. That happened with Arthur's buried treasure – Arthur put it on the table and I had to turn up my nose and say, "Get that out of here", and Martin and Vicki chorused together "Yes, sling it in the bin!" '

Another rule at *EastEnders* is that the children do not witness any loud arguments or fast action, nothing that could frighten them. They are always screened from this and the camera cuts away to them in a separate part

of the set. Some viewers thought that the child who played Annie, Mary's baby, was distressed through witnessing too much. 'She was simply not very happy to be around the studios,' said Corinne. 'There are not many three-year-olds who know they want to act, after all. It has to come from the parents.'

Sue Tully was aware of this in the scenes in which Vicki suffered from meningitis. 'Going to hospital – even if you're just acting – can be very frightening,' said the actress. 'What's lovely about working with Samantha is that she's always so happy. When she comes to work, she knows it's playing a pretend game, she knows my real name but she knows to call me "Mummy 'Shell" when the cameras are running. If she isn't involved for a couple of weeks, I like to visit her at home, so she's always relaxed with me. She has seen me in all kinds of situations but I didn't know how she'd cope if I cried over her.'

At Sue's suggestion, the BBC built a hospital room with the minimum of equipment. A consultant was present to check they'd got the details right and also to make sure neither the viewers nor Samantha were too distressed. The lively and healthy-looking tot still had to sleep in a large incubator with tubes attached to her body but, to the relief of Sue and Samantha's mother, she accepted this as part of the game. But the incubator was empty when Michelle's brave front cracked and she broke down. 'I insisted Samantha wasn't there when I had to sob,' said Sue.

Sometimes it's the real parents who are upset unavoidably. The parents of the baby who played the Osman's tragic cot death victim, Hassan, were understandably affected by the screen tragedy and upset that they hadn't been warned. This problem was avoided when Judith Jacob, who played Carmel Jackson, was able to act with her own three-year-old daughter, Aisha, and the writers obligingly called the young character, Darren's daughter, Aisha Roberts.

The adult actors have extra concerns, too, when there are baby scenes. Jan Graveson, who played Disa O'Brian, admitted she was petrified about holding the two babies who were cast to alternate in her highly emotional new-mother scenes. One baby seemed to like her but the other always took one look at her and yelled its head off.

But the producers make allowances for babies' off-days. Little Edward was teething on the day he was due to

Left: Vicki's first birthday.
Above: Ali and Sue with their new son, Little Ali.
Below: Disa rejected her baby at first but grew to love it.

be photographed for publicity shots with a special iced birthday cake. In recognition of his discomfort, the shoot was abandoned, the cake put in the deep freeze and a new date fixed when, happily, his gums were no longer sore.

Adam Woodyatt has memories of damp knees from holding baby Edward when they played father and son. But Michelle Collins was grateful to Edward for relieving her of having to wear again a red dress she particularly disliked. 'It was the one I wore for the wedding and the christening,' said Michelle. 'When Edward was sick over it, I knew it wouldn't recover and I kissed him for it.'

See how they've Grown

Far left: When the series began Michelle was still a schoolgirl.
Above: Sharon's come a long way since the days of her fluffy jumpers.
Top right: As he's grown up life has made Ian become tough, hard-bitten and ruthless.
Bottom right: Ricky's gone from schoolboy to married man in just three years.

69

Reigning Cats and Dogs

R oly the apricot poodle is an unsung hero of *EastEnders*. His owner, Dennis Watts, may have wished on occasions that he'd had a more macho hound – a snarling Rottweiler or pit bull terrier, perhaps, to chase off The Firm – but this poodle is nobody's toy. Besides, he matched Sharon's hairstyles so well!

Roly has been a bit of a rogue from time to time. He trampled over Tom's prize leeks for no reason other than, possibly, he felt the same way as we did about Tom's flat hat. That led to Tom stealing Arthur's leeks and winning first prize with them.

Usually Roly's behaviour is impeccable, though. He bit meanie McIntyre who was trying to evict Sue and Ali. He expressed all our thoughts when, after nibbling something tainted with rat poison in the foodstore, he chose to be sick in the perfect place – on Willmott-Brown's new carpet in The Dagmar. He was the first to find Pat in the gardens when she'd been savaged by the Walford 'Ripper'. Pat repaid him by demanding he be kicked out of The Vic when the Butchers moved in! Luckily Diane and Ricky changed her mind and Mo, who'd first suggested they get a kennel for him (a kennel!), warmed to him so much that he went to live with her for a while. Sensibly, Eddie Royle made friends with him when he came to The Vic. He now lives with Sharon there. Well, that's when he's 'at work'. In fact, he lives with the show's co-creator, Julia Smith, when off-duty.

Willy, Ethel's pug, is actually Roly's best friend. They share a dressing room and are always so pleased to see each other that they completely ignore the human stars of the show. Like Roly, Willy is not just a pretty, furry face, but has a proper role and has never been sentimentalised. He has been naughtier than Roly, though.

When Ethel was preparing The Vic food, Willy once ate all the expensive steak for the steak and kidney pies when her back was turned. Ethel replaced the meat with a less costly cut and everyone commented that the

70

Facing page: Debs with her kittens, Starsky and Hutch.
Left: Roly may not have lived up to Den's macho image of himself but he's been a good friend of The Vic's.
Below: Benny Bloom wanted Ethel but not if Willy came too.

pies were not up to standard. At Christmas 1990, he sneaked into the Fowler's kitchen and began scoffing the turkey. But Willy has been a victim, too. Kidnapped by an old man, he was found by Quick the copper in a pet shop. When Ethel fell and broke her hip, he went to stay with Dot and they each found the other a strain. Benny Bloom wanted Ethel but only if she was dog-free, and when Ethel and her pals went to off Clacton for a dancing holiday, Willy had to go too, in a holdall.

Cats haven't had much of a break in Albert Square. Marge was devoted to her mum's moggie, Tiddles: he was the one male in her life. Andy bought Debs two black kittens as a peace-offering after a row. He suggested she call them Starsky and Hutch because of her fondness for policemen. When Debs left she gave the cats to Sue Osman, but they brought trouble to the Osmans when the Health Inspector objected to them scuttling around in the café. What the Inspector never found, luckily, was Crush. This was the pet snake of Emine, Guizin and Mehmet's daughter. Because Mehmet had gambled away the family home, and the children and their mother were staying with Sue and Ali, the snake came too. In the crush, Crush escaped. It was Dot who discovered it: she had one of her turns. What became of Crush, we never learned. But some of the sausages Ali served up in that café looked distinctly, er, strange . . .

Living with Dirty Den

*T*he most famous rogue on television – lecherous, treacherous 'Dirty' Den Watts – was played by Leslie Grantham. The tall, gaunt-faced actor whose tongue is usually firmly in his cheek when talking about himself, grew up in St Paul's Cray, Kent, the son of a Boots The Chemist despatch clerk.

He left school at fifteen and, after a few different jobs, walked into an army recruitment office one day to avoid the rain and signed up. Little more than a year later, as a nineteen-year-old private with the Royal Fusiliers in Germany, he was given a life sentence (eleven years, as it turned out) for the murder of a taxi driver, a crime he has never sought to justify nor explain. In Wormwood Scrubs he watched a play called Norman, *badly performed by the inmates and helped by some professional actors and actresses who visited prisons. Leslie said:*

I was supposed to be auditioning for the part of Pete Beale, the fruit and veg man. It made sense because I'd worked in a green-grocers' in South Kensington when I was rest-ing as an actor. I was so used to weighing up apples and things that when I moved on to work in a men's clothes' shop, I kept making mistakes – licking my fingers as I wrapped up a shirt and twiddling the bag.

'I'd been recommended to Julia Smith by a director, Matthew Robinson, who'd used me in a stage play and in *Dr Who*. Apparently nothing registered with Julia at first, then she remembered she'd taught a mature student with that name at drama school.

'I had about an hour with her and Tony Holland and she said later that my knuckles were white with tension. I got a phone call

'Some chap came on as a toughie and I thought "I could do that".' And so he did, filling one of the vacancies created when two of the prisoners leading the drama group were sent away for electric shock treatment.

Among the visiting actresses were Louise Jameson and Pamela Salem, both of whom helped Leslie to apply for a place at drama school when he was released. Oddly enough, Pamela was auditioned for the role of Den's mistress, Jan, but the part went to Jane How. Leslie later persuaded the casting director to give her the role of Joanne, the hard woman who ran Strokes Wine Bar and eventually gave Den the brush-off.

Leslie worked his way through drama school, painting the VD clinic of St Thomas's Hospital in London by night. He took theatre work and small roles on television, including an army sergeant in The Jewel in the Crown. Then he was called to audition for EastEnders in 1984. He won a part but not the one he expected to get, and before he left in January 1989 he'd appeared in 410 out of the 418 episodes made up until then.

At his request, his shifty pub landlord, by then the sexpot of soap, was 'done in': shot by a hitman hired by local gangsters and left to rot in the canal until dredged up and buried a year later. Den may be dead but nearly three years on Leslie still hasn't lived him down and probably never will.

The actor, who's forty-four, has since starred in the ITV drama series Winners and Losers, two award-winning series of The Paradise Club for the BBC, made a successful West End stage debut in Rick's Café Casablanca and hopes to make a comedy series and much more before 1991 is out. He looks back fondly on EastEnders and the now legendary anti-hero he created. This is how he recalls his time in Albert Square.

that night to say they were considering me for someone called Den, a minor character – a bit like Dave in *Minder*, pulling a few pints now and then in the pub. She said the part would last about six months and I was hired for twelve episodes at just under £200 a week, certainly not the rate for one of the important actors in the series.

'I went back to meet the actress who was due to play Angie – Jean Fennell, it was then – and Letitia (Dean) who was to play my daughter, Sharon. I liked them and I liked the idea of the role. After six months, I thought, I could be off, doing something new.

'That's what I wanted. I never wanted a long run, I'm a shy, insecure bloke. When the BBC had the press launch for *EastEnders* everyone milled round Wendy Richard and Anna Wing and the other Fowler and Beale characters. I was pleased to be in the background.

'Anita Dobson was hired at the last minute in place of poor Jean Fennell. It wasn't her fault – anyone could have been changed; Julia was under such pressure to get things right. Jean was a good actress, but unfortunately her face just didn't fit.

'Anita, well, she grabbed it by the balls. She had such energy and charisma, nobody could mistake it. She lifted a mundane couple really out of the nether regions of Albert Square and into prominence. Because of her vitality and charisma Den took off. From the very first scene we did together – when she was planting a flower on a part of my anatomy and I had to carry her upstairs – I just knew the chemistry was right between us. Every scene with her was fun to do. In fact, it was great working with all the Vic crew – Tom Watt, Nick Berry, Letitia, Susan Tully and Anita. We all pulled together. Everyone had aggression; we moved around, and did things that I suppose were quite different, however ordinary they could have been. That's how we came to be called "The A-Team" on the show.

'But the main reason for the success of Angie and Den – this terrible, miserable couple – was Anita. She was paid more than I was – she was a late replacement and she had them by the short and curlies. But she deserved it.

'I decided to make Den as nasty as I could, meaner than the lines in the script. The biggest change was a scene in which Angie had a long speech about how she supposed it was all right for Den to have a mistress but that the boot was on the other foot if she had a fling with the Gala pie man. There were about four

pages of middle-class diatribe for me to come out with. It just wasn't Den. So I talked to Anita about it and I took a chance, replaced the whole speech with one word – 'Tough!' Apparently that made me loved and hated by every woman in the country.

'I risked other changes too – small things that came to me when the camera was rolling, but they worked. I made Den switch TV channels just after Angie had asked a very personal anguished question about their relationship. Another time I had him biting into a custard cream when she was really wretched.

'I suppose Den was at his most despicable when he gave Angie the divorce papers as a Christmas present. I actually suggested he put them in her cracker so that she'd be all excited, then get this horrible shock. But they wouldn't let me go that far. When I found out Den was to be the father of a schoolgirl's baby, it all started to happen. Den really was a bastard – it got me called 'Dirty Den', a name that's gone into folklore.

'Seriously, I'm really glad I had those scenes with Sue Tully as Michelle. If anyone deserves to be the star of the show, she does. It doesn't matter if she's speaking lines which make her really older and wiser than her years, she makes them believable and if you watch her you know she's such an intelligent actress.

'I'm really fond of Letitia, too. I'm sure she has a great future in musical comedy if and when she ever moves on. But the two of them used to drive me mad. They were always chasing me down corridors, throwing water over me before I was due to do a scene. And Tish is a terrible corpser – she'd always start me laughing when I was supposed to be dead sombre.

'Looking back, it was amazing that there were so few problems. I remember being furious when I'd expected to take a fortnight's holiday to coincide with Jane, my wife, having

There's a surprise in store for Angie.

Den, Angie, Lofty, Mo, Wicksy and Kathy get ready for another night in The Vic.

our first child, Spike. At the last minute I was told I was taking another sort of holiday – a trip to Venice with Anita for the show. I think I had four days off with Jane in the end.

'I told them in November 1987 that I wanted to leave and Den had to die. It had to be final both for my sake and for the sake of the rest of the cast. After all, everything you seemed to read in the papers about *EastEnders* concerned Dirty Den.

'Julia was shocked at first but I agreed to a storyline about the jail sentence that would lead up to the end slowly and allow new major stories to be developed. I'd always known that I didn't want to play Den for twenty-five years. I didn't want Den to end up another Ken Barlow, thanks very much.

'Banging Den up in Dartmoor – though we called it Dickens Hill – kept him alive for an extra year. It was the offer the BBC made me, a brilliant idea, and I'm very grateful for it. I didn't want to go in a way that harmed the show. This way I was able to record scenes for ninety episodes in five weeks. That must be a record. In the rest of the year I had time off to shoot a film, *Nightwatch*, for BBC Northern Ireland, then *Winners and Losers* for Scottish TV, and to make other plans.

'I was annoyed when I saw the death scene, and so was Julia Smith who'd directed it personally. Because I'd made it clear there would be no going back, I filmed Den collapsing from the bullet and tumbling into the canal. But all the viewers had was the sound of a shot and a splash; it was a deliberate tease. Julia was furious. She even had her name taken off the credits in protest.

'Since then I've been asked by viewers if I'm ever going back and I'm afraid the answer is no. Michael Ferguson, the current executive producer, doesn't believe in going backwards and he's right.

'Personally I can't see *EastEnders* will ever eclipse the days of 30 million viewers because those were heady days and the show was just not like anything else that had been seen then, especially on the BBC. No disrespect to the present cast – I really admire the way people like Wendy Richard and Bill Treacher have gone on and kept it fresh. The producers know the audience isn't going to take anything that's thrown at them out of habit. They're on their toes and I reckon the show is still going to get 20-odd million and we – you see, I still feel part of it – *they* are still going to make other soap operas pull their socks up.'

Who's Who

PAULINE FOWLER

It's been a life of drudgery, money worries and family tragedy for Pauline Fowler, but she keeps going, if not smiling. Her husband, Arthur, went to prison for fiddling the Christmas Club money; her sixteen-year-old daughter Michelle became pregnant by a man Pauline despised; her son Mark was involved with a married woman, got in trouble with the law and was sent to a detention centre. Pauline was sick with worry. Later, Mark tried hard to prevent her finding out that he was HIV positive.

Pauline conceived her third child when she was forty-three and was told by her domineering mother, Lou Beale, to have an abortion or else. Standing up to the formidable Lou for the first time in her life, Pauline said 'no', had her baby Martin and discovered a new strength.

When old Lou died, Pauline took over her role as the matriarch of Albert Square; Mother Courage in an Oxfam jumper. For her the family comes first, friends and neighbours second. The rest of the world comes a very poor third.

Arthur is her biggest burden. She sees him as weak and foolish, a man to be controlled with a hard stare and a sharp tongue, although Pauline loves him, in her way. Arthur proposed to her when she was ill in bed with the flu on the day she should have been a bridesmaid at her sister's wedding. If she hadn't felt so sorry for herself she'd probably have turned him down. After all, she dreamed of marrying a film star.

Pauline has had run-ins with most of the other Walford women. She finds it hard to forgive Kathy for leaving Pete Beale, her twin brother, and has fought duels with Cockney insults with Dot Cotton.

Even so, Pauline has a kind heart; she worried about gay Colin's problems when most of Albert Square decided they 'didn't want one of them living round here'. She tries to be tolerant of her daughter, Michelle, even though she doesn't understand her, and mistrusts that 'stuck-up' Rachel Kominsky and this back-to-college business. But the bond between them is as tough as steel.

Pauline worries about her health, and when odd things started happening to her she turned to alternative medicine, but it wasn't hypnotism she needed, it was a hysterectomy.

She's had a hard life, has Pauline, charring in The Queen Vic and washing other people's dirty linen in a very public launderette. She found life a bit easier when she had the job at Tates Paint Factory and a few bob coming in. And she needed no persuading to go into partnership with Kathy and Frank to run the café. But really she would like Arthur to get a proper job.

Pauline enjoys her cigarettes and her gin and tonic and the odd trip up-West. The troubles won't go away, but then Pauline is used to them. She's always known that life is a bed of nettles, not roses.

ARTHUR FOWLER

Sometimes you feel like giving Arthur Fowler a good shake. There's no harm in the man, he's a decent bloke who tries to do the best he can – but his best can be really exasperating.

How could he have been taken in by the Mitchell brothers like that, delivering illegal MOTs? A child of six would have seen that the Mitchells were bent, but not Arthur.

When he stole the Christmas Club money to pay for Michelle's wedding, Arthur was so incompetent at setting up a fake robbery to hide what he'd done that you wanted to shout at him. Pauline quite often does, and you can't blame her. But you can't be cross with Arthur for long; that would be like being mean to a small child.

Arthur had a nervous breakdown and was hospitalised; then he spent a month in jail for the Christmas Club robbery. His little pretensions are endearing and his small ambitions lovable. All Arthur wants is to make Albert Square green and lovely, to stand his round in The Vic, to grow a few new potatoes on the allotment, to see Michelle happily married, Mark on his feet and little Martin growing up to be a credit.

He can be a bit of a bore, going on about the state of his salvias, but he's soon forgiven. After all, Arthur hasn't had an easy life. He used to work in a toy factory but was made redundant and remained unemployed for years. Somehow, Arthur Fowler seemed to sum up the hopelessness of all Britain's

WENDY RICHARD

Few members of the cast were famous faces before EastEnders *began, but Wendy Richard is one of them. The whole country knew her as that flighty Miss Brahms from the BBC1 comedy* Are You Being Served. *Now America does too – the old shows are a hit there.*

She had been in show business for twenty-five years before the call came to put dolly bird parts behind her and take up the shapeless cardigan mantle of Pauline Fowler.

Born in Middlesborough, Wendy moved around the country with her parents, who were in the licensed trade. She was a favourite in films and television, notably the 1960s soap The Newcomers *and the comedy series* Dad's Army, *but is proudest of Pauline, whom she calls 'the salt of the earth'.*

Once out of Pauline's drab gear Wendy looks like a film star and is a WestEnder,

living in W1 with her third husband, Paul Glorney, and her pet cockatiel, Little Henry. She enjoys her beloved patio garden, tapestry and watching old movies.

But she's determined that Pauline will never become glamorous. There's only one bit of 'cheating': Wendy makes sure Pauline always wears rubber gloves to do the washing-up, so Wendy's nice nails are safe from the suds.

unemployed. For a time it looked as if he was going to do away with himself, but Arthur came through.

He still hasn't got a real job, though he is the official keeper of the Square's gardens. He worked in the shop for the Karims for a time, but they never trusted him and Mr Karim insulted him by offering a newspaper round. Arthur helped Pete Beale on the fruit and veg stall, and did a bit of this and a bit of that until he started to run errands for the Mitchell brothers.

Arthur will never make a businessman. He sold his and Pauline's share in the veg stall to Pete for three thousand pounds; he borrowed money from a loan shark to give Pauline a night out and was unable to comprehend the way the illegal interest mounted so quickly.

Even so, he's not all that dim, our Arthur. He can remember things, mostly useless facts, but he can remember. He won an exotic holiday in the TV quiz game *Cat and Mouse* and was the star of the quiz run by The Queen Vic. Perhaps he'll make a go of his jobbing gardener business, but you wouldn't bet a box of geraniums on it.

What Arthur Fowler cares about, in this order, is: Pauline; his children; his grand-daughter Vicki; growing plants; and Walford United FC. Most of the time he's happy, these days.

BILL TREACHER

Off-screen, Bill Treacher is nothing like downbeat Arthur Fowler: he's charming, self-confident and positive. You can't talk to him without sharing a joke and realising why he was once a hit with The Brian Rix Theatre of Laughter. Now fifty-four, he's happiest talking about his home life in Suffolk with actress Kate Kessey and their teenage children, twelve-year-old Sophie and sixteen-year-old Jamie, both of whom are mercifully free of the problems which beset the Fowler kids.

He cherishes his good fortune because times were tough when Bill was growing up in the East End during the war. After his National Service, he worked as a steward with P&O to save enough money to go to drama school where, ironically, he tried hard to lose his Cockney accent.

Bill had worked with Julia Smith and Tony Holland in Z Cars, and when they asked him to take a round-the-year-role in EastEnders and play Arthur who has a mental breakdown and a bucketful of woes, Bill held a family conference. The Treacher gang said 'Take it'. They were to suffer when the strain of the harrowing storyline took its toll on Bill. 'I once started crying when I was sitting at home in my armchair. I had to reassure my wife it wasn't me who was crying, it was Arthur.'

The sacks of letters he received from real unemployed, depressed people moved him greatly: but he's not cut out to be gloomy. You can usually find Bill on the EastEnders' set sending up his fellow actors and giving everyone the giggles.

MICHELLE FOWLER

Although Michelle may have done some silly things in her life, she's still smarter than the average EastEnder. She did well at school, and might even have gone on to university if she hadn't been made pregnant at sixteen by Dennis Watts. But even pregnancy couldn't keep her from her O levels; she took one examination in the maternity ward.

She's a determined girl, is Michelle. She ignored all the advice from family and friends to have the pregnancy terminated, and went on to give birth to little Vicki.

She made another mistake; she was talked into marrying Lofty Holloway, a nice guy but a guy she didn't, couldn't, love. She left him at the altar once, but finally sneaked off for a register office ceremony with him.

Michelle tried to make the marriage work, but Dennis Watts was just across the road and the torch she carried for him burned like an Olympic flame. Finally Lofty left her and the whole Beale–Fowler clan, and got out of Walford for good.

Later on, Den disappeared and all Michelle had in her life were her daughter and her family. She worked for Dr Legg for a time, took up hairdressing, typed for Walford Council and did a bit of temping before entering the shady world of time-share selling.

The three constants in Michelle's life are Vicki, her relationship with her mother, which is sometimes stormy but always steadfast, and her enduring friendship with Sharon Watts. These two have been best friends since schooldays and the only serious rift came when Michelle made the mistake of

SUSAN TULLY

One of the outstanding young actresses on British television, Susan Tully is an old hand in the business at twenty-four. At the age of nine, she hosted Our Show, *which went out live, worked on* The Saturday Banana *with Bill Oddie, then played Suzanne in* Grange Hill *for four years.*

At that stage, acting was only a hobby, but Sue says she never felt she could leave Michelle in the studio at the end of the day. The two young women have something in common. Sue has a working-class London background, her father was unemployed for some time like Arthur and her mother had a baby late in life. But Michelle's run of bad luck has never worn Sue down. 'I've grown up with Michelle; she arrived in her school uniform and she's been through pregnancy, a marriage and divorce and taken all sorts of knocks. She's changing fast now. But thanks to her I've been half-way round the world, I have a lovely flat, tremendous freedom and the chance to work in a series which tackles difficult issues in a way I'm proud of.'

Sue has filled her time away from Walford with many different projects, including supporting The Meningitis Trust, running in the London Marathon to raise thousands of pounds for charity, playing in both the football and cricket EastEnders' cast teams to raise money for charities and, in short breaks, performing in stage plays.

telling Sharon that Dennis Watts was Vicki's father.

Both Michelle and Sharon were distraught at the time about Den's death. Michelle mistakenly thought that Sharon would welcome the news that something of Den lived on in Vicki. But Sharon broke from Michelle completely, seeing the relationship with her father as a betrayal. Eventually they became faster friends than ever because this pair need each other's emotional support.

Michelle feels she needs a man but she is far too independent to repeat the Lofty Holloway mistake. She did fall for Danny Whiting, a married computer engineer, and even lived with him briefly when his wife threw him out. (Danny claimed he'd done the leaving.) But that went wrong, too.

Michelle has always had the feeling that her life should be broader, more interesting. She's always been afraid of slipping into domestic drudgery in the same way her mother did. So when she moved into Rachel Kominsky's flat, Michelle was excited – if worried at first – to meet the feminist lecturer's clever friends. Now she's a mature student at the Poly. It's tough. So what's new?

Michelle's horizons are widening and it couldn't happen to a nicer girl.

MARK FOWLER

Mark is Pauline and Arthur's eldest child – and their most difficult. He broods a lot and communicates little. Although he loves his parents he fails badly to show it. He and his sister Michelle mean a lot to each other but it's a spiky relationship; they often exchange harsh words.

TODD CARTY

Before he zoomed into Albert Square on his motor bike as runaway Mark Fowler in the summer of 1990, Todd Carty was a schoolgirls' heart-throb as Tucker Jenkins in Grange Hill *and later in* Tucker's Luck.

This caused problems because Mark had previously been played by David Scarboro. But that young actor found the strain of being in a smash-hit soap, and having his own life compared with that of his screen character, too hard to take. He left the series in 1987 and in the following April came the sad news that David, suffering from depression, had committed suicide by hurling himself off the cliffs at Beachy Head. He was only twenty.

Although a photograph of David as Mark remained in the Fowler's sitting room, few viewers and none of the cast expected the character to return. Todd was allowed to re-create the role only after David's real parents gave the idea their blessing. He fitted the role because he looked as though he could be related to Sue Tully, who plays his sister.

There was something harder in store: Mark was to reveal to his girlfriend Diane that he has the Aids virus. 'I had my own fears, knowing the stigma attached to it all. It's almost like saying I have the fatal disease myself – I have to handle the public's reaction.'

Luckily that has been positive so far and Todd, who likes snooker, football and tinkering with motor bikes and cars, is cautiously hopeful that he has helped to open a few closed minds with his performance.

As a teenager, Mark was involved with Nick Cotton, Dot's criminal son, in some shady dealings. Pauline has always felt guilty about Mark; she feels that by spending so much time fighting to get a living she and Arthur failed to give the boy the love and attention he needs. Michelle feels a sharp sibling rivalry. To her, Mark has always been her mother's favourite.

Mark left home and failed to get in touch, leaving Pauline and Arthur worried to death. Finally they tracked him down to Southend where he was living with an older woman. That relationship broke up but Mark continued to drift around, a dosser on a motor bike. He spent time in a detention centre after getting into trouble with the law. Pauline visited him and begged him to come home.

Her pleas fell on deaf ears. When he was released Mark continued to drift for a couple of years. Finally he came riding back into Albert Square, hiding a terrifying secret behind a black visor.

No one could fathom what was wrong with Mark until he broke down and confided in Diane Butcher, who had fallen in love with him. Diane had gone walkabout too, living on the streets for months, and she understood his insecurities. Mark confessed to her that he was HIV positive and Diane tried hard to help him.

She even persuaded him to see a counsellor but Mark turned on the man. All his bitterness at being a potential Aids victim poured out. He had caught it from a girlfriend, but the disease, he shouted at the counsellor, was 'spread by gays like you'. Diane kept Mark's secret. He loved her for it and wanted to marry her. Disa, her streetwise friend, found out by accident. Now Rachel, who fancies him, has found

out too.

Mark Fowler is a genuinely tragic figure, full of hate and anger, but unable to show it.

PETE BEALE

 Rough and ready, that's Pete Beale. Rough with his tongue and his fists, and ready to jump into an argument whether he knows anything about it or not. Act first, think later, if at all, is Pete's attitude. He wouldn't get into Mensa – he'd have trouble filling in the application form.

Pete may seem to be as thick as a brick, but he *is* a brick. To people he loves, anyway. He loved his old mum, he's fiercely protective of his twin sister Pauline or any other Beale, and he cares about Albert Square and the people who live there. And he'll never stop loving Kathy, who left him because he didn't understand why it took her longer than five minutes to get over being raped.

Pete's not sure how he feels about his son, Ian. He wants the boy to be macho, to do what a man's gotta do at all times. He pushed the reluctant lad into the boxing ring, and he was all for Ian sorting out Wicksy with his fists when Wicksy stole Ian's wife, Cindy. Pete was beginning to feel proud of young Ian's business brain and the way the boy's catering business is growing. But he can't stomach the lad's calculating ruthlessness.

Pete Beale had his dreams, too. When he was a young tearaway, running around with Den Watts, Pete saw himself as a singer, a Butlin's redcoat and a hotel owner.

But he's always going to be a barrow boy, supplying Albert Square with fruit and veg.

He's reasonably honest, not slipping too many rotten apples into the bags. The Beales have been running that stall for a very long time and family pride plays its part.

In 1963, when he was eighteen years old, Pete married Pat Harris because she said she was pregnant. As it turned out, she wasn't. To the Albert Square boys in those days Pat was a slag, but a man's gotta do . . . Pat already had a child by someone else and a couple of years later Pete left her when she was six months pregnant with Simon (Wicksy). He thought he was the father. Years later he discovered he wasn't.

Three years after leaving Pat, Pete married Kathy, in the face of Beale family opposition, and thought he'd live happily ever after. But he never really understood Kathy, and never responded to her sensitivity nor her aspirations. And the aftermath of the rape caused her to leave him. Pete took to drink, almost became a tramp and faced two drink-driving charges, but he pulled himself together.

Now he's a lonely man. A romance with New Zealander Barbara never took root and Pete misunderstood the signals when that forthright lecturer Rachel Kominsky seemed to be friendly. So far, the women he has met through the dating agency make him lonelier still. Will he ever find a woman to replace the gap left by Kathy?

KATHY BEALE

When you consider the hard life she's had, Kathy Beale has turned out very well. Blonde, good-looking, intelligent and industrious, on the surface Kathy's a together lady.

Underneath, though, things are very different. Kathy had a difficult childhood. She came from the slum

PETER DEAN

When Peter Dean landed the part of stall-holder Pete Beale, he didn't have to do much research. Peter's family had a stall in Chapel Market, Islington, for years and he was 'discovered' while spouting Shakespeare in Petticoat Lane one Sunday morning. The actress Prunella Scales was passing and advised him to take drama classes.

Peter's grandmother was the music hall artist Lily Randall, and she taught him the speech from Antony and Cleopatra *that Prunella heard. (Peter was flogging sheets at the time.)*

From then on his life was divided between acting and street-selling jobs until the acting took over. He appeared in Law and Order, *Coronation Street, Target, Minder, Shoestring and many more programmes.*

Peter was born in Hoxton fifty-three years ago, and knew the Kray twins as a lad ('nice enough fellas'). He has been married twice, has a daughter of twenty-two, and practises a Japanese form of Buddhism – a far cry from prosaic Pete Beale.

end of Walford and her family was the poorest of the poor. Her father drank, her mother was terrified of him, and there was never enough money to go round.

Then, when she was fourteen, Kathy was raped. She became pregnant and her daughter was adopted. Later on, when she could face men, she fell for Pete Beale. But Pete married Pat Harris, who said she was pregnant by him, and it was only after Pete walked out on Pat that he and Kathy finally got together.

They married and produced little Ian. Kathy felt she'd left her unhappy past behind her at last. Pete was doing well with the fruit and veg stall and Kathy went into business with a knitting machine, producing one-off jumpers.

Then she made the mistake of going to work in The Dagmar, an upmarket pub run by the equally upmarket James Willmott-Brown. Willmott-Brown fancied her and

Kathy liked him, even though she was always completely faithful to Pete. One night, after closing time, her boss raped her in the room over the bar.

Kathy's world collapsed. To be raped a second time made her wonder if there was something about her that was 'asking for it'. Pete blazed with anger, of course, but the anger was as much against her as the rapist. She had also to cope with Donna, a difficult, drug-taking girl who turned out to be her daughter, the product of the first rape.

Everything became too much for Kathy. Her marriage to Pete broke down; she just couldn't live with him. Kathy went through a further ordeal when Willmott-Brown finally came to trial. She had to give evidence against her former boss and a skilful barrister presented a good case for him. For a time it looked as if he would be found not guilty, but eventually Willmott-Brown went to jail for three years.

GILLIAN TAYLFORTH

The part of Kathy Beale nearly didn't go to Gillian Taylforth because she was too pretty. Finally it was decided that there are good-looking girls in the East End so why not on the show? Gillian's another real Londoner, and her father is a printer, her mother an office cleaner.

For years Gillian worked as a secretary between acting jobs. She claims that she's not a very good actress, but anyone who watched her handle Kathy's rape ordeal knows differently.

Gillian went to the Anna Scher Theatre School and appeared in many films and television shows. You saw her in Hi-de-Hi, Shelley, On Safari, Sink or Swim *and* The Rag Trade. *She lives in North London, rather too close to where the* EastEnders' *cast football team used to play: they would invite themselves in for brunch after each game and eat her out of house and home.*

For a time, Nick Berry (Simon Wicks) was her boyfriend, but now her partner is businessman Geoff Knights. The couple are delighted that their first child is expected in 1992.

Since then Kathy has tried to put her life back together, but there have been more problems. When her son Ian was involved in a fearsome car crash she went through agonies. Kathy tried to help Ian sort out his troubled marriage to Cindy, but eventually Cindy went off with Wicksy, taking with her Steven, the 'grandson' Kathy had come to love so much.

Now past forty, Kathy is an attractive, bright, caring (she's a Samaritan) and highly moral woman, vulnerable but tough in some ways, streetwise, amusing, even witty, though she still can't learn to button her lip. What she thinks is what she says. If Frank Butcher thinks he can lord it over her as they run the café, he's mistaken.

For a time it looked as if Kathy had found the right man in Laurie Bates, a rival to Pete in the market, but in the end she decided to hang on to her independence. Eddie Royle, landlord of The Queen Vic, was interested and Kathy found him a nice guy, but so did other women.

IAN BEALE

 Once quiet and caring, Ian Beale has become the sharp businessman of Albert Square. The son of Pete and Kathy, Ian has developed his catering business from a mere sandwich round to a thriving posh nosh operation in what used to be The Dagmar. He used to own the Square's café, which he took a notch upmarket from its 'greasy spoon' days of Ali Osman. Ian went to catering college and he's always been clever with cash. As a teenager he loaned money at interest to Ali and Mehmet Osman to finance their gambling.

Ian had to grow up too fast. Pete was always on at him to become a man, to do well at boxing, to experiment with girls. Kathy had grander ambitions for him and he seems to be achieving them for her. But at some cost; Ian Beale has become hard. When he was younger he gave his uncle, Arthur Fowler, money to get a loan shark off his back. He cared about people.

Today's Ian wouldn't do that. His self-inflicted car crash, and the desperate fight with Cindy and Wicksy for custody of his son Steven, have left him bitter. His motto now seems to be 'Ian Beale against the world'. Planting stolen goods in The Dagmar to get the squatters evicted showed Ian at his very worst.

ADAM WOODYATT

So many strangers stopped Adam Woodyatt in the street or at traffic lights to tell him his 'missus' (Cindy) was 'having it off' with his best friend (Wicksy) that he lost count of them. But Adam didn't blame his screen wife Cindy for her agonising infidelity: he rated his character Ian Beale as a bit of a plonker at the time. 'Now I've got another name for him – swine', he joked.

Adam, unlike Ian, is neither an innocent nor furiously ambitious. He began acting as a child growing up in Chingford and had just started his first job after school, working in a butcher's, when Albert Square beckoned. He's been a member of the EastEnders cast since the beginning.

He lives near Elstree, has a steady girlfriend and a sunny outlook. If it all ends tomorrow, Adam won't complain. The role has enabled him to buy his own home at eighteen, a fast car, and indulge his passion for Paintball – war games to the uninitiated.

This new toughness has made him a better businessman but a less attractive human being. Maybe the right girl will soften him up a little, though Ian has never had much luck with girls. He went out with Sharon Watts for a while but she soon showed she preferred the more experienced Wicksy.

For a short time he lived with a girl called Tina but her parents found out and Ian had to go back home. There were other love-life failures too but young Ian thought things were going right when he realised that Cindy Williams was interested in him.

He couldn't know that she was using him to make Wicksy jealous. And when Cindy agreed to marry Ian, the groom had no idea that the child she was carrying was Wicksy's.

For a time he was happy with Cindy. He was working hard at the business, Cindy was helping and when little Steven was born, Ian's cuppa flowed over. Until, that is, Cindy left him for Wicksy and he finally had to accept the fact that Wicksy was Steven's father. Cindy and Wicksy left Walford and now Ian doesn't even see Steven.

But he's got his thriving business empire to keep him warm. If the bookies ever start offering odds on who will become Albert Square's first millionaire, put your money on Ian Beale.

LOU BEALE

A frightening old woman, Lou Beale was an East End matriarch who terrorised both the Beale and Fowler families and most of Walford as well.

Her twin children, Pauline and Pete, were well scared of her. Their elder and smarter brother Kenny had the sense to get away and emigrate to

ANNA WING

When Anna Wing became a national figure as matriarch Lou Beale, she was seventy-one. It wasn't exactly an overnight success: Anna had been an actress almost all her life, although she started out as an artist's model.

'Lou made me better known than anything I'd done in fifty years,' said Anna. She's a genuine East Ender herself and turned up for her audition clutching her birth certificate to prove she was a Hackney greengrocer's daughter.

During the Second World War, Anna worked in East End hospitals. She was married at thirty but got divorced three years later. She had a long relationship with the poet, Philip O'Connor. Anna lives in Brighton, is a left-wing sympathiser and a CND supporter.

Since leaving the series in June 1988, Anna has worked on stage and television. She especially enjoyed playing the medium, Madame Arcati, in Noel Coward's comedy Blithe Spirit.

New Zealand. Only Michelle stood up to her gran and, perhaps because of this, Lou had a soft spot for her.

Lou mellowed a bit in later years, though she was still hard enough to tell Pauline to get rid of a late baby and vicious enough to taunt Arthur about failing to find work.

Even Big Pat went to see her when summoned and that was really something, because Lou always maintained that Pat had tricked Pete into marriage many years before. But she had her good points too: she was understanding during Michelle's pregnancy and Arthur's breakdown.

Dot Cotton and Ethel Skinner, being

contemporaries, were able to deal with her as equals, but even they felt the force of old Lou's displeasure keenly.

When she was cross you could run a deep freeze for a year on her facial expression. But when she died in her sleep from a long-term heart condition and went to join her dear husband Albert in the cemetery, there was hardly a dry eye in the Square. They still talk of her with a catch in the throat. Maybe it's simply a case of distance lending enchantment to the shrew.

FRANK BUTCHER

Ex-landlord of The Vic, Frank Butcher is a big man, physically. And he'd like to be thought of as a Big Man in business – an operator, a wheeler-dealer, a guy with stacks of business credibility.

Frank started out as a used-car salesman with a wad of notes in his back pocket and a line of chat that ran a lot more smoothly than some of his old bangers. Then he met up again with barmaid Pat Wicks (*née* Harris), with whom he'd had an on–off liaison (they met at Butlins in Clacton in 1958) for thirty years.

Pat was working at The Queen Victoria and Frank, whose wife June had died after producing their four children, soon moved in with her.

He opened a used-car lot in the Square, they managed to get the pub's licence jointly, and they got married, even though Pat suspected that all Frank really wanted was a mother for his children. They worked hard, adding a small bed and breakfast hotel to the businesses they ran, until they decided they had taken on too much. So they gave up the licence of The Vic.

MIKE REID

Believe it or not, Mike Reid, who plays Frank Butcher, was once a Hackney coalman. Then he discovered a talent as a stand-up comedian and left the nutty slack behind him.

Mike always wanted to be an actor rather than a comedian but 'having started a family at seventeen and never having the chance to go to drama school, I had to kick that idea into touch.'

He first appeared on television in 1972 in The Comedians, *had a Top Ten hit with 'The Ugly Duckling' three years later and worked a lot in television.*

Mike has been married to his wife, Shirley, for more than thirty years, though both had been married before. He's had real tragedy in his life. His son, Mark, killed his best friend in a mock duel. Later Mark killed himself and four months after that his twenty-three-week-old daughter Kirsty (Mike's grand-daughter) was found dead in her cot. Obviously such things leave deep scars. But Mike's a pro: he knows you go on with the show and you keep the gags coming.

The Butchers have been happy together, finding a kind of middle-aged contentment after both leading stormy and eventful lives. Not that their married life has been entirely smooth. Big problems have arisen, mostly concerned with their children.

Frank's youngest, Janine, was a problem child who wouldn't take to Pat. Frank was persuaded to attend a Child Guidance Clinic with the family but he hated the idea. He didn't believe an outsider should even know about Janine's difficulties, let alone help to solve them.

His middle daughter, Diane, seemed a happy enough girl until she ran away from home and lived rough with a gang of dossers for months. Frank was in despair, wandering around London searching for her, until she phoned from Kings Cross and asked him to bring her home.

Mo Butcher, Frank's old mum, came to live with the couple and caused a lot of upsets because of her interfering ways, then finally was diagnosed as having Alzheimer's Disease, which explained a lot.

Frank used to be a bit of a wild man, but he's kept out of bother in recent years. He's still likely to go off for a night's gambling, though, and he'll still sell you a dodgy motor if you're not careful.

PAT BUTCHER

Without doubt, Pat Butcher is the most forthright woman in Albert Square – and there's plenty of competition for that title. 'Big Pat' is a tough enemy, a good friend, a straight talker, a flashy dresser and a woman you don't tangle with.

She's settled down since she married

PAM ST CLEMENT

Big Pat Butcher is a joy to play, according to Pam St Clement. She laughs at the tarty clothes Pat wears, and the way her mouth opens before her brain is engaged, but she understands that the woman had been hurt by life and doesn't want it to happen again.

Pam is forty-eight, divorced, and never thought she'd end up as an actress. She was big in the drama society at her boarding school but thought she'd become a vet or a journalist. She hung about London 'sampling life' in the Swinging Sixties until she went to a teacher-training college.

After that it was drama school, but Pam did earn her living as a teacher for a short time. But it couldn't last. The acting bug suddenly bit and Pam was away. She worked

extensively on the stage, in films and on television in such programmes as the Onedin Line, Private Schultz *and* Emmerdale Farm *before arriving in Albert Square.*

Frank and become a little softer. But it doesn't take much to reveal the old battling Pat who lurks under the surface. When her son Simon and his girlfriend Cindy were fighting the Beales for custody of baby Steven, Pat was right there for them, punching her full weight.

Pat Butcher has more past than a history book: her life story would make at least three thick novels. Born Pat Harris, she emerged as a looker in her early teens, and at the age of sixteen she won the Miss Butlins title at Clacton.

Frank Butcher was there with his girlfriend, June, soon to become the first Mrs Butcher. But after the beauty contest Frank went with Pat to Chalet 204 and they made love. She told him he was the first.

Then June got pregnant, Frank married her and Pat began playing the field. The pair met up from time to time, and on each occasion the affair would be rekindled. But Frank wouldn't leave June, and Pat lost count of the men she slept with trying to rediscover the rapture she'd found with him.

The nearest she got to it was with Dennis Watts, though he was chasing Angie even then, and Kenny Beale – both of them restless men unwilling to settle down.

Kenny Beale's younger brother Pete married Pat when he thought she was pregnant. She wasn't, and old Lou Beale always believed it was a deliberate ploy to trap Pete. Yet Pat couldn't settle down and eventually Pete left her.

While they were still together, Pat had two sons, David and Simon, both by a man named Brian Wicks, even though Pete thought Simon (Wicksy) was his. There was a messy divorce and eventually Pat married Brian. She stayed with him until he started knocking her about. Then she came to Albert Square, met up with Frank again, got a divorce – Brian demanded a car as payment for letting it go through – and eventually married Frank. For a while she seemed content to run the B & B. But housework is not her style. Flirting with the customers in The Vic is what she's good at.

Although Pat has mellowed a bit and people like and trust her more, there are still not too many folk in Albert Square who'd care to get on the wrong side of Big Pat.

DIANE BUTCHER

The best-looking member of Frank's brood is his daughter Diane. For a time she was also the least troublesome, and the one who conformed the most. But she fell in love in a schoolgirlish way with a young building worker called Paul Priestley. He first had a brief affair with hairdresser Julie Cooper, then went back home to Leeds. Diane began to think that nobody loved her.

On her sixteenth birthday the family pretended they had forgotten the day, because they'd really planned a surprise party. But the scheme went wrong. Already emotionally disturbed, Diane decided that no one cared and ran off into the night.

She lived rough on the streets of London for three months and joined a gang of dossers, when she was befriended by a girl called Disa O'Brian. Diane tried to grow a hard shell but failed. Eventually she rang her father and asked him to come and fetch her. For once, Frank restrained himself and welcomed her back with love and sympathy, not hard words. Diane refused Mark Fowler's offer to settle down. Now she's showing her independence by working in France.

What he didn't know was that Diane had met a photographer named Taylor who took nude pictures of her and used them to construct a life-size sculpture. She thought it was a work of art but when it turned up in Albert Square, Frank went wild.

The first real adult love affair in Diane's life was with Mark Fowler, and that was never consummated because he was HIV positive. Diane gave Mark strength when his bitterness and anger ('Why me?') were making his life almost impossible and he was talking about suicide. By the time he was strong enough to talk about marriage, she wanted to leave Walford again, this time for France.

Diane can be a bit of a pain when she gets too intense, but at heart she's a nice girl.

JANINE BUTCHER

She's a little horror, is Janine, though she's slightly less horrific than she used to be. When Frank's first wife June died, Janine was only four. At first she lived with Frank's eldest child, Clare.

Then Frank brought Janine to live at The Queen Victoria – and the child went berserk. No one could deal with her; not Pat, not Frank, not even his tough old mother, Mo.

Janine screamed, refused to eat, ran away.

Eventually Frank agreed to a session at a Child Guidance Centre, and although he refused the therapy offered, the Butchers did pick up a few tips on how to live with Janine. Maybe she'll settle down in time.

SOPHIE LAWRENCE

It was literally by accident that Sophie Lawrence, who plays Diane Butcher, became an actress. She wanted to be a dancer but tore a muscle in her groin and was told to give it up. So she turned to acting, went to drama school, and went from there straight into EastEnders. She is only nineteen.

When her character had to live rough for three months, Sophie did some research among the real homeless, became worried by their plight and vocal on their behalf: she's a girl who cares. She has worked on children's television shows, and plans to marry young and have her own children. Not your typical teenager, Sophie doesn't drink and can't get excited about going to clubs.

She admits she's a touch bossy, which is probably why her long-term aim is to be a theatre director.

RICKY BUTCHER

'Thicky' Ricky has learned a lot in a few months, all thanks to a pretty girl who needs him – Samantha. He failed all his GCSEs, but then no one ever accused the boy of being an academic.

Ricky helped out his father Frank on the car lot for a while and did some stupid things. Things like showing off by driving a car before he'd passed his test and knocking down Pauline Fowler in the Square. He was fined seventy-five pounds and had his provisional licence endorsed.

He soon got over that, because he was becoming besotted with Shireen Karim, but her father was determined nothing should come of that relationship. Eventually the Karims shut up their shop and moved on.

Ricky showed some talent at mending cars, so the Mitchell brothers took him on at their auto repair shop. At first they treated him with a heavy hand, but lately they've begun to see him more as a younger brother. They don't want him mixed up with any of their dubious goings-on.

Even so, they were suspicious of him whenever Ricky went out with their much younger sister Samantha. The Mitchells were as jealous of her virginity as the mafiosos they'd like to be. If they'd seen Ricky's comical fumbling with her they might not have worried. When the young pair defied orders and ran off to be married, the Mitchells accepted Ricky. Perhaps they realised Sam had made a man of him.

SID OWEN

When the EastEnders *credits roll, they say that Sid Owen plays Ricky Butcher, but he isn't really a Sid – he's a David. When he was younger, he was a bit of a podge, a pudding, so his friends nicknamed him 'Kidney', as in steak and kidney pudding. Kidney became Kid, which became Sid, and the cheery nineteen-year-old accepted it.*

Sid was a child actor who appeared in Oliver Twist *at the age of nine. Then came drama school and* EastEnders *two years ago. He met Nick Berry's sister, Amanda, at Nick's twenty-fifth birthday party and now they are engaged. A big thrill was taking her to New York to meet his pal, Al Pacino, whom Sid got to know when he had a small role in the movie* Revolution.

Sid loves football, riding his Yamaha 125 motor bike, listening to Motown and swooning, jokily, over Kylie Minogue. He doesn't drink but he does eat more than anyone else in the cast. IQ note: Sid is at least twenty times brighter than 'Thicky' Ricky.

SAMANTHA BUTCHER

A teenage tease, Sam is a pretty girl who thinks she can get anything she wants, thanks to her own brand of sexy wheedling. It certainly works very well with love-struck Ricky Butcher; Sam manages to twist him around all her fingers and not just the little one.

She's a lot sharper than her brothers, Phil and Grant, and contrives to do just what she wants in the face of their attempts to stand in for their dead father. (Sam was a young girl when he died.)

Sam did well at school without working too hard, and liked going out to clubs because when she's wearing make-up she can add two or three years to her age. Her reason for running away to stay at the garage or at the Butchers' used to be that she couldn't stand her mother's new man, Kevin. This may well have been an excuse. Sam loves excitement and doesn't frighten easily.

She's a user, able to get almost anyone to do what she wants. More than one East Ender will be fascinated to see how Smartypants Sam develops.

MO BUTCHER

When she arrived in Albert Square, Mo's new neighbours viewed her as a tough, interfering busybody with a will of iron and a face of stone. Only slowly did Walford begin to see a softer side to hard-bitten old Mo.

Frank's mother was born in Walthamstow

DANNIELLA WESTBROOK

In a way, Danniella Westbrook rolled into the part of Sam Butcher. Aged eleven, she had been thrilled to get a day's work as an extra, as a kid roller-skating her way across Albert Square in front of her idols, Den and Angie. When the local paper published Danniella's picture and ran the item, the punchline was 'Who knows, one day she may be the show's star!'

That day came just as the pretty Essex teenager, who'd persuaded her parents to let her attend stage school, was finishing her History GCSE exam. 'I put my pen down and I think I ran all the way to the audition, in my school uniform,' she said.

Danniella thought she had no chance as she'd only appeared as a model or in commercials before. 'But they told me they were looking for someone bright and bubbly, who could be the sister of Phil and Grant, and my round face fitted.' Now eighteen, she loves her work but disapproves of Sam's forwardness. And much as she likes Sid Owen, who plays her husband Ricky, she's happy with her kitten and her long-term boyfriend, Kevin. 'I've no plans to settle down,' she said.

and still sees that borough as the centre of the world. As a youngster she married a man, nicknamed Chike, who had worked for London Transport since he left school. When he was finally made an Inspector at the age of forty-five, Mo felt she had achieved some status at last. She was proud to be an Inspector's wife.

She had two children, Frank and Joan. Joan, the elder, was also the brighter of the two. Joan managed to get seven O levels, one A, got a job in a bank and married a chief accountant. More status for Mo.

But when Frank became a licensee he too had climbed up the ladder, so Mo moved into The Queen Victoria with him. She thought she was going to be Queen Bee,

EDNA DORE

Actress Edna Dore, who played poor senile Mo Butcher, is alive, well, living in Barnes with her stage director husband and working on the West End stage. Edna, who is now seventy, began her career as a chorus girl in ENSA, then spent twenty years in rep before being a member of the National Theatre for ten years. Although she longs to play grand ladies in beautiful clothes, she liked Mo the battleaxe in the battered hats, and was pleased to be able to help people understand how Alzheimer's Disease afflicts the strongest amongst us.

Edna was also at home in The Vic, then owned by her screen son Frank, played by Mike Reid. Edna sometimes lends a hand at her real son Mike's Sussex pub or plays a game of cards with her teenage grandson, rather as she did between the scenes with Sid Owen, who plays her grandson Ricky. 'I'm not brilliant behind the bar but I used to pass on Mike Reid's jokes to my Mike to pass on to his regulars,' she said.

and regarded Frank's new wife Pat as nothing more than a pushy interloper.

All of that left Frank in a very tricky situation. Gradually some sort of compromise was worked out and slowly old Mo became more human. To her grandchildren she was always indulgent, but to Frank she was always the boss, a woman with a whim of iron.

For a time Mo took over Walford Brownies – and what a handful they were – when Brown Owl Marge could cope no longer. But Mo had to lie about her age to get the job and eventually the Girl Guide HQ caught her out, so she had to resign.

Perhaps it was just as well, for not long afterwards the first signs of a mystifying forgetfulness began to appear in the old woman. Eventually, after she had caused a flood at the Queen Victoria, she was diagnosed as suffering from Alzheimer's Disease. Daughter Joan arrived to take Mo to live with her in Colchester and both Frank and Pat shed a quiet tear.

In fact there was hardly a dry eye in Albert Square at the departure of a woman they had first seen as a scary old battleaxe. It just goes to show, you can't judge a book by its cover.

SHARON WATTS

 There's a lot of her mother in Sharon Watts. There is the warm sympathy and the barbed tongue for a kick-off. But Sharon is more sensible than Angie, less likely to fly off the beer handle in The Vic. All the same, she's a sensitive, vulnerable girl who is easily hurt.

Even so, that doesn't stop her going after something she really wants. It was Sharon who insisted on a second search of the canal, the one that finally yielded up Den's body for a decent funeral. And her pursuit of Grant Mitchell, far too much of a Jack the Lad to see himself at the altar up till then, may still be a story of persistence rewarded.

It is surprising that young Sharon, adopted at the age of three by warring parents Den and Angie, grew up so well. A pub isn't the perfect environment for a youngster; a pub run by that pair could hardly be a worse one.

Yet Sharon came through it to become a very nice girl behind the streetwise image. She didn't fare very well with the male sex: Ian Beale was too green, Dog Collar Duncan too earnest, Wicksy too much of a wanderer. Only time will tell if Grant is really Mr Right or Mr Hopelessly Wrong.

When Angie went away Sharon developed a strong need to track down her real mother, though enough people warned her it would end in tears. Undaunted, she finally found Carol Ann Stretton, happily if boringly married to Ron Hanley. At first Carol didn't wanted to be reminded of a youthful mistake, especially one her husband didn't know about. But eventually she and Sharon came to an understanding, each happy to have found the other.

Michelle Fowler is the important, steadying influence in Sharon's life. The two friends are like sisters and, like sisters, they sometimes fight.

Sharon's lost a bit of weight since her puppy fat days, and with her blonde hair and bright make-up she adds a cheerful touch to drab Albert Square.

LETITIA DEAN

If her life had been as difficult as her character Sharon Watts', Letitia Dean reckons that she'd have 'jumped in a lake by now'. Thankfully, unlike adopted and rejected Sharon, the pretty blonde actress gets on well with her supportive parents, whom she often visits at weekends. Her mother, Doreen, even lends moral support when Letitia makes personal appearances. 'She's great, I can always count on her,' said the actress, who was only sixteen when she began in the show.

These days, Letitia shares a West End house with her actor brother, Stephen. They used to do a dancing act together and on one holiday weekend in Blackpool won no fewer than four talent shows. Letitia was in the musical Annie at the age of twelve, and she also sang with a rock group, The Young 'Uns. Music is still

important to her and she enjoys the times when Sharon is allowed to sing in The Vic. She also manages to squeeze in a few weeks of pantomime each Christmas.

Letitia's close friend on and off screen is Sue Tully, and they share a dressing room. 'Sue's calm and laid-back, ideal for me because I used to be a bit hyperactive.'

She can be tough – she has Angie's knack of breaking up a pub fight before it starts – but she's terrible with money.

As for work, Sharon did a YTS stint in a supermarket, helped in a travel agency and then came full circle to be barmaid at The Vic. She took Eddie to the Industrial Tribunal when he sacked her. Now she's taking them all on for The Vic itself. Den wouldn't half be proud of his 'Princess'.

PHIL MITCHELL

The cooler of the two Mitchell brothers, Phil is also the elder by two years. He and his brother, Grant, are very similar – both stocky, crop-haired and with a sense of physical danger about them. Their late father had a big local reputation as a boxer, and both boys are handy with their fists.

Yet neither of them are the hard men they like to think they are. Their auto repair shop under the railway arches may front some illegal goings-on, but Phil's only police record is a few drunk-and-disorderlies and a taking-and-driving-away.

Phil is the thinker of the Mitchell double act, and if he's not exactly an intellectual at least he can sum up any situation in a couple of sharp phrases. He's the most streetwise of the pair and, judging by some of the shady deals they get involved in, he needs to be.

He wasn't keen on Sharon's closeness to Grant. Real concern that she could not cope with his moods? Or a touch of jealousy? Phil needs a woman too.

GRANT MITCHELL

Always ready for direct action, that's Grant. He's only too happy to duff someone up or sort someone else out, and look what he did to Eddie Royle when the late landlord of The Queen Vic apparently trespassed on his patch. Usually, though, Grant's big brother Phil restrains him; he knows they have to live in the real world, not some East London version of Chicago in the 1920s.

Grant joined the army to see the world, but having seen Cyprus, the Falklands and Germany he dropped out, just as he had dropped out of school. The scars of war go deep. He still has bad nightmares, terrible rages. Still, he did a mechanic's course in the army and that's come in useful for the car repairing trade.

Both Mitchell brothers like girls, drinking, clubbing, gambling, living on their wits and laughing at Walford. If what they're doing is no longer fun, the Mitchells want to move on. If only Grant had moved on from cursing Eddie Royle in public, the police

ROSS KEMP

'Pretty tame' is the way Ross Kemp, who plays volatile Grant Mitchell, describes himself. A London policeman's son, he has certainly never been in a fight, unlike Grant, who is given to violent outbursts. The only rough stuff the twenty-seven-year-old keep-fit fanatic indulges in is on the rugby field. He still plays for Maidstone and this summer, with Leroy Golding, set up the EastEnders' cricket team which plays monthly games for charity.

Ross paid his way through drama school by working as a waiter and a labourer, but his stocky build and receding hairline were already earmarking him for future roles as coppers, villains and, in Emmerdale (as in EastEnders), former soldiers. Ross, who's unmarried, enjoys working with Letitia Dean, who plays Sharon. 'Grant was a bit of a tart, but he really loves Sharon,' he said. 'For ages he couldn't bring himself to say so, though.'

might have left him alone. Instead he was a prime suspect for murder.

Young Sharon Watts has managed to slow Grant down and it seems she'll get him to the altar, but no one believes the wild days of Grant Mitchell are over. Not by a long chalk.

PEGGY MITCHELL

Peggy Mitchell is the mother of Phil, Grant and Sam, and you can see where the boys get their toughness and Sam her knack of getting her own way. Peggy is now in her mid-fifties but likes to think she looks much younger. She's flash, fast-talking and nobody's fool. She has always done things her way and heaven help anyone who crosses her, though her bark's usually worse than her bite.

She's proud of her home. It's always spanking clean, the knick-knacks are always gleaming and everything's as new as possible. She married her late husband, Eric, a boxer, because she was pregnant with Phil. It wasn't the glamorous life she'd hoped for

and she thought about leaving when the boys were teenagers. Then along came Sam, an accident, and she had to stay, even though she rather resented Sam because of it. Later she met Kevin, her current boyfriend, when she went to work for his minicab firm and made a play for him. They had a secret affair but Eric developed cancer and Peggy gave up work to nurse him. They had to draw the dole, which she hated.

Kevin came on the scene so promptly after her dad's death that Sam took against him, even though there was money in the Mitchell home again. Phil and Grant don't care for him either.

DOT COTTON

A born victim is the only way to describe Dot Cotton. With each blow that life delivers she bobs back up again, almost asking for more trouble, more pain, more suffering. But nothing shakes Dot's view that the world is good because the Creator made it so.

Her faith sustains her through the most

appalling ordeals. Charlie Cotton, the man she married at twenty, forced her to have an abortion a year later and threatened to leave her if she didn't. She shouldn't have agreed because Charlie left her anyway; at regular intervals over the next thirty years and then he finally disgraced and humiliated her with a bigamous marriage.

He wasn't around when their only child, Nick, was born. At the time, Charlie was living with Dot's half-sister Rose in Liverpool. Only her close friendship with Ethel Skinner – though sometimes it seems to be based more on hate than love – has kept Dot going through the terrible years.

That and her faith.

Nick developed from a nasty schoolboy into a fascist thug, a liar, a cheat and a jailbird, often conning his mother and stealing money from her. Eventually, when God finally smiled on Dot for her years of devotion and allowed her to win ten thousand pounds in a bingo game, Nick tried to poison her so he could inherit the lot. Later, he became a heroin addict.

Various lame ducklings have been mothered by this old duck of a Cockney lady. Donna, the child of Kathy Beale's teenage rape, used and abused her before she died from a drug overdose. Rod the

JUNE BROWN

Actress June Brown, who plays daft but lovable Dot Cotton, claims she is lazy, but for a lazy woman she's done an awful lot of work. For a long time June was a member of the prestigious Royal Shakespeare Company, and her film and television credits would easily fill a page of this book.

June lives in Croydon with her actor husband, Robert Arnold, and their cats and dogs, although their five grown-up children are in and out of the house all the time.

June, now fifty-seven, has had a lot of sadness in her life. Before she was sixteen, five close relatives had died. And her first husband, another actor, killed himself because he thought he was seriously ill.

June lost a premature baby and her daughter, Chloe, was born paralysed, although miraculously she was cured by the age of two. Chloe gave June her first grandchild, Matthew. Perhaps that's why June, who can be just as chatty as Dot, can, unlike her character, smile most of the time.

Previous page: Ricky and Sam Butcher married in haste – are they now repenting at leisure?
These pages: The up-and-down relationship of her parents has taken its toll on Sharon Watts. Her relationship with Simon Wicks fell apart when he realised he still loved Cindy Beale. Will there finally be a happy ending with Grant Mitchell?

Life has dealt Dot Cotton some heavy blows but she's always struggled through. Her son Nick has progressed from bad to worse to downright wicked and her late husband Charlie seemed determined to humiliate her. At least her cares and woes haven't dulled her enjoyment of gossip. Dot, her best friend Ethel Skinner and old Lou Beale *(below)* used to make a formidable trio, though there've been lighter moments too, such as the Ladies' Darts Team trip on the Thames *(facing page)*, when a good time was had by all.

Although officially niece Vicki *(facing page)* and uncle Martin *(above)*, the two latest additions to the Fowler family are more like brother and sister. Both babies were accidents, but happy ones as it's turned out. *Over page:* Baby Stephen with his parents Cindy Beale and Simon Wicks.

punk accepted her help and did manage to give her something back in the way of warmth and understanding. Hazel started out by conning Dot, but ended by liking and respecting her.

And Disa the dosser, who had a baby by her perverted stepfather, can thank Dot Cotton for keeping that baby alive. She stood up to the bully and got the tiny child away from him as he threatened to dash it to the ground. She deserved a medal for being so brave.

Dot will go on providing Albert Square with a conscience, combining the roles of silly old woman and near-saint. Dr Legg will never cure her hypochondria and Dot will never cure her smoking habit. She'll probably go on believing that Nick can be redeemed. It seemed she would carry on working in that run-down launderette until the last clapped-out washer went into its dying spin. Now it's the B & B she'll work in and worry about. And all the while, the essential riddle of Dot Cotton will remain unsolved: how anyone so exasperating can be so lovable.

CHARLIE COTTON

 This was a man who gave parasites a bad name. As cunning as a fox and as slimy as a snail, lorry driver Charlie arrived in Dot Cotton's life at intervals to give her grief. Even so, she always forgave him, even though she always knew it would end in tears when Charlie filched what he could and moved out once more.

He regularly two-timed Dot with her half-sister Rose and then betrayed both of them by bigamously marrying a woman called Joan from the Midlands. It's hard to understand why any woman was taken in for ten seconds by the nasty little man, but he must have had some sort of charm.

Charlie performed just two good deeds in his life, which ended when the lorry he was driving crashed during the summer of 1991. He promised Dot a new gas cooker and actually bought it for her when he came by some money. And he tried to save her from the poison trick of wicked Nick. It's not much to set against a life of scheming and double-dealing, but it's better than nothing.

NICK COTTON

 Even worse than his trickster father, Nick is the most malevolent man ever seen in Albert Square. Rapists, arsonists, murderers, con men and thieves regularly turn up there, but none of them has ever been as irredeemably wicked as Nick, Walford's very own Prince of Darkness.

The glitter of evil makes him attractive in a loathsome kind of way. Dressed all in black, he seems to flit on the scene like a vampire bat and flit out again when he's sucked up enough blood.

It is tempting to blame his parents – Dot for spoiling the boy rotten and Charlie for never being there as Nick grew up – but there is never any real explanation for genuine evil. It simply exists, and Nick Cotton personifies it.

He graduated from truancy to small-time crime, to violence, to heroin abuse and drug dealing, to blackmail, to racism with a skinhead fascist organisation. He's tried burglary, pimping, passing stolen cheques, beating up girls . . . You name the crime,

Nick's committed it. He even confessed to Dennis Watts that he beat pensioner Reg Cox to death, though he was never brought to trial for it.

Nick usually goes on the run after pulling a criminal stroke. He beat up Hazel, then disappeared and did not see his mother again until she had her ten thousand pounds bingo win. Then he arrived claiming to be a born-again Christian, blinding poor Dot with smarmy fake religiosity while he sprinkled her shepherd's pie with poison.

When heroin almost killed him in the summer of 1991, his mother rescued him again. Again he lied to her. Again he tricked her. But not even he was prepared for what happened when he met Eddie Royle on that fateful September night. Will he lie his way out of this? Or run away again? However much inflation devalues our money, there will never be a bad penny worse than Nick Cotton. He'll probably keep turning up. Rubbish like him always does.

ETHEL SKINNER

Dot Cotton's best friend and dearest rival is Ethel Skinner. The two have known each other forever and love each other dearly, but they can't spend more than five minutes together without bickering.

Ethel is a game old bird, giggly in drink, and still with a glint in her eye under her terrible ginger wig whenever a good-looking man passes by. (She and Dot got really snappy with each other when they squabbled about an Over-Sixties dancing partner.)

Walford is full of survivors but Ethel takes the championship crown. One night in the Blitz a bomb hit Ethel's house when she was

JOHN ALTMAN

The mildest man in the cast, banker's son John Altman had been out of work and on the dole when the role of twisted creep Nick Cotton came up. Before meeting the producers at the BBC, he psyched himself up at a 'greasy spoon' café in Shepherd's Bush market. 'I was pretty obnoxious at the interview,' he said. 'I wanted the part badly, so I gave the character all I'd got. I'd never been so aggressive in my life.'

Whereas racist Nick would kill his mother for her bingo winnings to buy dope for himself or sell it to children, John is devoted to his mum Tina, his wife, Asian actress and model Brigitte and their daughter Rosanna, five, and has never been tempted by drugs. He was appalled when he researched the depths to which real addicts sink in preparation for the 1991 heroin story, the hardest yet in his playing of Nick's nightmarish life. Nick's matted hair, dirty clothes and make-up-department-produced rotten teeth were hard for the almost fanatically hygenic John to bear. But he hopes he has been convincing enough to deter people from experimenting with 'smack'.

John, thirty-nine, who studied photography before deciding to follow his grandfather Johnny Scofield Jnr into acting, is a keen guitarist and song-writer who'd like nothing more than to record an album. In his spells away from Albert Square, he has been busy on stage and in television, including a spot as a head-banging rock guitarist in The Paradise Club *with Leslie Grantham.*

'Being known for Nick Cotton can be frustrating,' he said. And funny. When Nick was pretending to have found Jesus in jail, he was pictured on the front of The War Cry, *the Salvation Army magazine. They thought he was Saved. How wrong can you be?*

out and all her family were killed. Since then she's battled on alone, with only Dot, her awful dog, Little Willy, and memories of jiving with glamorous wartime GIs to keep her going.

For a time she was engaged to Benny Bloom, an old friend of Dr Legg's, but backed out when she realised she couldn't take her precious Willy to live in Benny's place. Later on she was told that Benny had died and left her two thousand pounds, but his daughter contested the will for a time.

Ethel is a lot sharper than she looks. She was the first to suspect that Nick Cotton was trying to poison his mother, though Dot didn't thank her for it.

Ethel's malapropisms are wonderful: when she was sent off to live in a 'sceptred housing' flat she went with a smile, declaring herself 'quite continent'. Ethel represents the old Walford, when the place was an underprivileged urban village and everyone knew everyone else. It's hard to imagine the Square without her Donald Duck voice, sharp eyes and indomitable spirit. Secretly, Dot hopes she'll live forever. Being Ethel Skinner, she probably will.

DR LEGG

The man who knows more about the people of Albert Square than anyone else is sage old Dr Harold Legg. After all, as he's fond of pointing out, he brought half of them into the world.

There was a time when Dr Legg thought he was getting too old for general practice but the mood passed. Maybe he's not so well-versed on the newest drugs as younger medical men – though he has a keen interest in social medicine – but he does understand that a doctor's most useful service to his patients is reassurance.

He is kind, caring, funny in a dry way, but sharp enough to spot the malingerer and wise enough to humour the hypochondriac.

Albert Square trusts Harold Legg and Harold Legg loves Albert Square. It's an unsentimental kind of love, not expressed with much tenderness, but nevertheless it's there and Albert Square knows it.

It's been there since his schooldays. His Jewish family got out of the East End when

GRETCHEN FRANKLIN

As befits a former chorus girl, cabaret and musical comedy performer, Gretchen Franklin, who plays Ethel Skinner, has lovely legs and dancing feet. One of the most popular members of the cast as well as a favourite with the fans, she has done everything in show business except appear in a circus. 'I should have done, all my mother's people were in that line. My grandmother used to ride a horse round the ring, juggling,' she recalls.

She might have been a household face sooner

if she'd retained her role as Alf Garnett's 'Silly old moo' of a wife in the original comedy play of Till Death Us Do Part.

Like busy-body Ethel, Gretchen loves animals and is Vice President of her local branch of the RSPCA in Richmond, Surrey. But Willy the pug doesn't go home with her.

'I tried to buy him from the BBC but he's too valuable now, he earns a bomb in personal appearances,' she said. Besides, her own dog, a pooch called Urnay, would not approve.

Mosley began his marches. They moved to Finchley, but young Harold travelled from there daily to his East End grammar school, so as not to mess up his education.

He went to Bart's to start his training in 1940, treated air raid casualties, and met and married a non-Jewish nurse. They bought a cheap little house in Albert Square and would have lived happily ever after, if a random German bomb hadn't killed Harold's bride.

He has never remarried, despite the hard work of matchmaking aunts. Dr Legg has just got quietly on with his task of keeping the Square healthy.

He's had his lapses, of course. He failed to diagnose meningitis in Michelle's baby Vicki, for instance, and the child almost died. But Harold Legg is a wise and good man. The Square is lucky to have him.

LEONARD FENTON

Wise Jewish doctor, Harold Legg, is played by Leonard Fenton, who grew up in the East End and qualified as a civil engineer before he turned to acting in such series as Z Cars, Colditz *and* Secret Army. *He also played the Austrian Jew, Erich Gottlieb, in the long-running* Shine On Harvey Moon.

Married to cellist Madeline Thorner, Leonard is a highly cultured man, a talented artist and (to the amusement of his fellow actors) a master of dog impressions. One reason his appearances in EastEnders *are limited is that he suffers from diabetes and a condition, sometimes called apoplexy, which can cause his muscles to go alarmingly limp for a few moments. He loves to exchange jokes – but laughing can suddenly bring on this distressing problem.*

DR DAVID SAMUELS

While he worked with his uncle, Dr Harold Legg, Dr David Samuels suffered chronic irritation, which was a shame. David, who came from Israel, joined the older doctor when the young Sikh assistant, Dr Jaggart Singh, moved on at Christmas 1987 to a job up north. But despite being truly fond of each other, the new partners argued about almost everything: computers; David's familiarity with Michelle (who was their receptionist at the time); Legg's lack of persistence over Donna's drug problem; and the older man's refusal to tell Colin Russell that he had multiple sclerosis. When David's pretty girlfriend, Ruth, arrived on a visit, David decided they should marry and return to Israel together.

CELESTINE TAVERNIER

The award for being the most upright, law-abiding citizen of Albert Square must go to Celestine Tavernier, but he doesn't get much thanks for it. Now in his late forties, he was born in Trinidad and raised by his grandmother after his mother died and his father Jules left to find work in Jamaica. He came to Britain in 1966, recruited by London Transport, with the intention of studying at evening classes for a white-collar job. He achieved his ambition, conformed and worked hard. He is now rightly proud of his respectability, his decently-mannered children, his bright wife Etta, their comfortable council home, his job as a manager at the Walford DSS and his standing among the folk at church.

He's not a happy man, though. He knows his father thinks he has lost his roots. His older son Clyde thinks he has 'sold out' and accepted the prejudices of his bosses who've been slow to promote him. His twins wish he'd loosen up and get excited about something other than their school reports and the cricket results.

Celestine has learned to live with East End racism, although his Albert Square neighbours have always been cautiously friendly. He can cope with the friction and tension in the house, Lloyd's illness and his father's often irritating ways. He has even come to terms with what he sees as Clyde's lack of ambition.

It's his relationship with Etta that's the main problem. He loves her and has always been loyal, but when she decided to push ahead in her career he began to feel slighted. When he booked a trip to Paris but she chose to attend a course instead, it sparked off a big row. When they discovered she was pregnant, Celestine assumed Etta would have the baby and put her ambitions aside. He found things weren't that simple. No wonder the hero-worship of young Yvonne from church seemed so comforting. It's only recently that Celestine realised he had to change or he'd be the loser.

ETTA TAVERNIER

A busy bee, that's Etta. She's always been the real boss at home, clever enough to let Celestine and Jules believe they were the heads of the household, and strong enough to cope when Lloyd's sickle-cell anaemia gave her nightmares and rebellious Clyde left home.

Etta married Celestine and gave birth to Clyde in Jamaica, then came to England to join her husband. It was a time when most West Indians were expected to work on the buses or in hospitals and not to be ambitious. Life was hard at first but they pulled together. As he plodded away and won a clerk's job, then climbed a few rungs up the ladder, her instinct was to train for a job she knew she could do well and enjoy – teaching. She followed her hunch, pausing when the twins were young and whenever Lloyd was ill, and never letting work come before the family's needs.

When the council rehoused the Taverniers in Albert Square, Etta was delighted that there was room for Clyde to come back to

LEROY GOLDING

Now forty-one, Leroy Golding came to London from Jamaica at the age of eight, and says he was a bit of a tearaway as a kid. He became a social worker, then joined a photographic agency, appeared in advertisements, did stunt work and played a policeman extra in EastEnders. *His acting career took off after he read for a small part in a Channel 4 play,* A Sight Better Off, *and was given the lead role.*

Playing respectable Celestine Tavernier means Leroy must wear a straight face and straight clothes six days a week – something new to him.

'He's serious, I'm a serious raggamuffin' he jokes. 'I've grown my moustache and cut my hair but I still sympathise more with the kids who waste their time and get into trouble.' No doubt, Celestine would not approve.

live with them. She smoothed over the clashes between him and his father. When Clyde brought his own little son Kofi into the fold at Christmas 1990, she was even more pleased.

Then her work threw up a new challenge – the chance to apply for the headship of Walford Primary School – and Etta's life seemed to be richer than ever. Excitedly, she applied for the post and got the job.

Etta decided to be positive about her health and sought an operation for sterilisation. Perhaps she already knew the price would be Celestine's male pride. He seemed to resent her success. Her unexpected pregnancy plunged everything into turmoil.

Telling Celestine about it was bad enough. The strain of having the test for sickle-cell anaemia in the foetus was worse. Learning that the result was positive and opting for a termination was worse still.

Like all the women of Albert Square, Etta has learned that you can't have it all.

JULES TAVERNIER

Living in Albert Square is more enjoyable than Jules would care to admit. He likes being a 'character', enjoys turning on the charm to Dot Cotton and Ethel, and raising his hat to all the ladies with a smile and a twinkle in his eye. He's not a moaner and his old-world flirting makes a pleasant change.

According to Jules, Trinidad is the only place to be. Give him half a chance and he'll tell you the history of the Caribbean in 225 chapters. Officially, he's only in Britain on holiday, of course. It started in 1968 and he stayed on to help look after newborn Clyde so that Etta could do her teacher's training and then teach part-time. The truth was he had nothing much to go back for. His wife had died young, he'd never settled in Jamaica and when the twins came along he had a full-time job helping the family.

Because he never went through Celestine's struggles for acceptance in a white community, he doesn't understand his son. He has more in common with the children, and especially with Hattie who shares his impish sense of humour. He loves drinking rum or Guinness, meeting his pals, singing and, as a gambling man, he's in his element when Eddie Royle's dad John turns up. If Ali and Mehmet Osman were still around, there'd be a card school every night.

CLYDE TAVERNIER

Clyde has never accepted that black people have to tolerate prejudice without protest. This was always one cause of the rows between him and his father. And when he began working behind the bar at The Vic and money went missing, he was furious to be suspected. Clyde had good reason to feel bitter, thanks to years of being harrassed by the police. Yet he had never once broken the law.

After he left home he took odd jobs, lazed around, did a bit of boxing and impressed a few girls. He met Abigail and they had a son but then split up. She moved to Bristol where her parents lived. When she was killed in a car crash two years ago, they looked after the child, Kofi.

Suddenly older and sadder, Clyde tried harder to find satisfying work and enough

money to visit the boy. A temporary job on a council play scheme introduced him to youth social work. He now does it on a casual basis, and attends college part-time. He knew he had to act when Abigail's parents planned to take Kofi to live in the West Indies. He argued with them until they took him seriously and he brought the child home to Walford.

When he arranged joint outings with Michelle Fowler and Vicki, Michelle hoped he was also interested in her. It seems she was wrong.

Tackling troublemakers at The Vic, he showed the Mitchells he could fight. They tempted him back into the boxing business and bruised him in more ways than one. His manager said he lacked the killer instinct.

STEVEN WOODCOCK

Not only does Steven Woodcock play Clyde Tavernier in EastEnders, *but he also appears as Jevon, a mate of the Trotters, in* Only Fools and Horses. *He's twenty-seven, unmarried, lives in Hackney and was in the same* Grange Hill *year (playing Rasta Glenroy) as Sue Tully, who plays Michelle Fowler. Steven started as a writer and one of his plays,* Gah-Gah Reached the Top, *was performed at London's Royal Court Theatre. He has appeared in* Casualty, London's Burning, Rockcliffe's Babies *and several other television series.*

Steven was once a keen boxer, which came in handy when Clyde took up the sport in 1991. A serious musician, he has composed over 150 songs and plays the guitar and bass professionally. He plans to use some of his EastEnders' *earnings to build a recording studio in his London home.*

Sometimes he lacked sense, too. He panicked when he found Eddie had collapsed, injured. Then he went on the run.

LLOYD TAVERNIER

Like Clyde, Lloyd was named after one of Celestine's cricketing heroes. But Lloyd will never become a sporting champion, partly because his inherited illness, sickle-cell anaemia, makes him prone to bouts of tiredness and weakness and partly because he'd far rather be a rap or rock musician or an artist. Now in his mid-teens, he happily helps around the house, listens to his grandfather's stirring tales of the independence struggles 'back home' and hangs around with the local kids.

Lloyd's no high flyer at school and depends on his twin sister, Hattie, to help him. He hates having to take things easy, and when he tried to do a paper round and ended up in hospital, exhausted, he showed the strain of having a disease that could mean a short life.

HATTIE TAVERNIER

Hattie is almost too well-balanced and happy to live in Albert Square. She loves music, sport and could have a string of boyfriends but, unlike Sam Butcher, she's not yet interested.

Clever at school, particularly at science, Hattie looks up to her big brother, Clyde, and protects her twin brother, Lloyd, who is slower and quieter and can seem a bit of a wimp. She even let her own schoolwork slip

GAREY BRIDGES

He may only be twenty-one but Garey Bridges, who plays Lloyd Tavernier, has already taken a big knock in life. He wanted to be a dancer but was told bluntly at fourteen, 'you're too small!'

'At the time I was shattered,' he said. 'But I went to stage school and when I began to hear my voice in bits and pieces on television, I started to get the buzz. I've danced with Wayne Sleep in The Hot Shoe Show *and I'm determined to stick at dancing, along with acting, whatever they say.'*

MICHELLE GAYLE

Fans of Grange Hill *will remember Michelle Gayle, who played Fiona Wilson while studying and passing her GCSEs and A levels. Now she plays the happy Hattie Tavernier. She loves singing and hopes to develop a separate career there. 'At the moment I sing with two boys in a rap band called R-MOR-FUS in odd clubs and places,' she said. At twenty, Michelle loves playing younger parts and finds having Garey Bridges as her screen brother a great bonus. 'It turns out that he and I know the same crowd of people in North London so we are often out together at night.'*

at times to help him.

Bossy, giggly and garrulous, she was an instant success helping as a waitress at Ian Beale's functions, even though it caused her parents distress. Hattie is as bright as her mother and loyal to her father. When her parents were quarrelling she was deeply upset, but nothing can dampen her natural good humour for long.

EDDIE ROYLE

The most serious-minded landlord of The Queen Victoria, Eddie Royle came into Albert Square as a man with a past, a man making a new start and keen to get things right. Eddie was friendly, a good listener to his customers and, for most of the time, a good organiser of his staff. But he was always guarded, reserved, and not the sort Pete might tell a dirty joke to or Dot confide in over her latest health worries. He was somehow a bit old for his forty odd years.

Born in Ireland, Eddie came to Britain with his parents as a boy. Bright and energetic, he couldn't wait to join the police and when he did, he loved his job, priding himself on being an honest copper. When he moved to the Serious Crimes Squad, he saw how corruption seeps in, how basically decent officers come to falsify reports when they're sure a man is guilty, can't quite prove it but need results. He was certain then that his boss, Dave Penton, was honest and when he decided, after long heart-searching, to report on the wide-scale corruption going on around him, the hostile reaction to him for 'letting the side down' shocked and surprised him. He stayed a further two years, despite being treated as a traitor, before taking early retirement. In 1990 an inquiry into police corruption sucked him back in and, when his former colleagues threatened to harrass him until he lost his landlord's licence, he tracked Penton down and found that he'd been 'on the take' all the time.

Eddie liked The Vic, liked the fact it's not a plastic palace and that the customers look out for one another. He was determined not to allow anything 'iffy', so he rejected Frank Butcher's offer to fill him in on how to fiddle the brewery, and he wouldn't stand for any drugs or deals in items which had fallen off the backs of lorries.

He was moral, sensitive, could be romantic and often he felt deeply lonely. He didn't marry when he was a policeman

MICHAEL MELIA

His battered nose may make Michael Melia, who played pub landlord, Eddie Royle, look like an ex-boxer, but actually he's an ex-teacher who's never been in a fight in his life.

The hooter was shattered three times: Michael fell off a trolley at the age of five, bashed his nose on a gate and finally came a cropper playing football.

Michael, forty-five and born in Berkshire, has been acting in television since the early 1970s, usually playing heavies or policemen, though he spent four years doing the classics with the National Theatre.

At one stage he ran a bar in Spain and thought about applying for the tenancy of a pub over here, like his character. However, the idea was vetoed by his wife, former actress turned teacher, Celia (who first turned him down when he proposed because of what her married name would be).

Michael's years in Spain left him fluent in the language, so he can enjoy the dubbed version of EastEnders shown on Spanish television. 'The same actor does about four of the voices. When those characters are all in a scene together, it's hysterical!' he laughs.

because he'd seen his mates' marriages buckle under the strain of police life and end in divorce. In Walford he decided he needed a mate. He patiently pursued Kathy and was especially tolerant, for her sake, of her son Ian using The Vic as the loading bay for his private catering jobs. But after a few dinners together Kathy gave him the brush-off.

When Sharon seemed to be opening her heart to him and was fed up with Grant, he rashly offered himself as a replacement. Grant steamed in after closing time and beat him up. He got his health back within weeks. Getting his 'bottle' back to take control took longer, and he sulked upstairs as chaos reigned in the bar. While he was in hospital, his pretty friend, Eibhlin, returned to see him. He saw her as the answer.

He thought he was right to sack Sharon when she allied herself with Grant – in Eddie's eyes, a villain. He knew he was right to ask Eibhlin to be his bride. But there was nothing right about the violent way he died.

JOHN ROYLE

Eddie Royle's father, John, is a wily Irishman. Now a widower, he's a retired metal worker who was a schoolboy international footballer and could have played professionally if he'd wanted to leave Dublin, which he didn't. He can be the life and soul of any party, and was the perfect pal for Jules Tavernier and Ethel Skinner. Sometimes, though, he can be quiet and impenetrable. John was very proud of his son and wouldn't get mixed up in anything that would have earned Eddie's disapproval. The shock of Eddie's death is something it will take him years to get over.

EIBHLIN O'DONNELL

Eibhlin worked wonders for Eddie Royle's image when she first visited him in Walford. The pretty, elegant, warm-hearted Irish woman met Eddie Royle in London about ten years ago. He was attached temporarily to the police PR department, and Eibhlin's job for the Irish Tourist Board in Dublin took her to the London office for a six-month stint.

Now in her mid-thirties, she was thinking about settling down, but she loved her job and the social life that went with it.

Eibhlin is still firmly committed to her close-knit Catholic Dublin family, especially her widowed father and Maureen, her unemployed, pot-smoking younger sister.

Eddie liked her intelligence and her sense of fun, and they always had good times together whenever she was in London. They'd never discussed marriage until 1991. But she managed to transfer to the London office and the pair began to plan a future together in Walford. A part of her was never quite convinced it would work. Now that Eddie is dead, Eibhlin will never have to put it to the test.

RACHEL KOMINSKY

The title of Albert Square's most tactless resident goes to Rachel Kominsky. Educated and cultured, she is currently confused about her real ambitions and needs. Originally, her family came from Eastern Europe. They're Jewish and arrived when Mosley's blackshirts were on the march in the 1930s. She teaches English and history on a Women's Studies course at a large polytechnic and has cut down her hours so she can try to develop her writing.

Rachel moved into the Karims' house after splitting up with her builder lover, Russell, with whom she'd lived for seven years. She left him because it seemed to her he was turning into a conformist and, as she cruelly told him, a bore in bed.

To pay the sizeable rent, she needs a lodger. Michelle mistook Rachel's polite, casual manner for instant acceptance as the tenant she needed. Rachel back-tracked when Michelle mentioned little Vicki, a child who could cramp her social style.

But her first lodger, singer Karen, didn't stay long and Rachel was only too pleased to offer Michelle a room after all. Considering they're chalk and cheese they are good for each other. For Rachel knows little about the real East End and upsets her neighbours by spouting her opinions at them. Perhaps she should watch more television and stop pretending to despise it.

At the moment what she doesn't want is a permanent man. But although she dresses like a student and her hair is usually untidy, Rachel is attractive and she likes a drink. There are a few Walford men who reckon they're in with a chance. One is Mark. He makes her happy despite everything. Will Rachel find he disproves all her theories?

DENNIS WATTS

 The late landlord of The Queen Victoria, Den was the most powerful character Walford has ever seen. He was also a much more complex man than he appeared on the surface.

Dennis Watts was flash, hard, aggressive, bloody-minded, highly attractive to women, mysterious, tough, a loner and a right

JACQUETTA MAY

The call to Walford came when Jacquetta May was half-way through dancing a tango. She almost had to say no to the role of Rachel Kominsky because of it. Jacquetta, who plays Rachel, said: 'It was a very odd project I was contracted to finish, all about the Argentinian tango, which a group of actors were improvising and which would have gone to the Edinburgh Festival. It looked as if I wouldn't be free in time to accept. But then the EastEnders *people allowed me to come a day later, so I was able to finish.'*

The Kent-born actress had worked in theatre for ten years after leaving Bristol University, with one short television role as a vengeful wife in *The Bill. On stage she'd played Rita in* Educating Rita, *Lady Chatterley and all sorts of roles at the National Theatre.*

So far, Jacquetta's enjoying the fact that she's rarely recognised. 'I can sit in a café and read a book without anyone asking me what'll be happening next', she said. 'But I do like Rachel. A lot of the stuff she talks about I recognise. I can't bear her when she's being priggish, though. Yet I loved it when she announced flatly she wouldn't have a television set, then went upstairs to sneak a look at Michelle's. She might well turn out to be the character you love to hate.'

bastard. He was a man with a villainous past, a murky present and, as it turned out, not much of a future.

He was also devoted to his family, capable of unexpected acts of generosity and understanding, and loyal to his mates. Den had a code of conduct all right, though it didn't coincide with Britain's legal code all that often.

Almost universally, women fancied him but were repelled by his uncompromisingly macho persona; an odd amalgam of lust and disgust. Den thrived on it. He never cared too much what other people thought about him, went his own way, did his own shady deals, and ran The Vic and his private life like an autocrat.

His relationship with his wife, Angie, was a roller coaster of passion and poison, intense love and hateful rows. They met at school where he was a trainee tearaway and she was developing a reputation as a scrubber. They married young but it soon turned sour.

Angie was ambitious. She wanted a bigger car, a better house, flashier clothes, a touch of class – or what she thought was class – and Den wasn't making money fast enough for her. There was a sexual problem, too. Soon after they married Angie rejected him and Den became bitter. He turned, of course, to other women.

His mistress, Jan, was several cuts above him socially, a bit of smooth, but she couldn't take his lifestyle. Her successor, Mags, accepted the lifestyle but couldn't take the attitude that went with it: 'I'm the man and you do what I say.'

Michelle Fowler was a one-night stand whom Den slept with simply because she was there. She loved him but he developed feelings for her only after she bore his child.

The most important person in Den's life was always his adopted daughter, Sharon. He called her 'Princess' and treated her like one, but he had to be the Emperor. If she spoke out of turn he rewarded her with a slap round the chops and he watched over her virtue like a rabid Dobermann.

Den had always been on the wrong side of the law, but when he moved out of his class and began running drugs for the Walford mafia, The Firm, he moved on to the direct road to hell. After his divorce from Angie, they put him in to manage a wine bar/gambling den and when he double-crossed them they had him murdered. Shot by an assassin, he fell into the canal by the spot where he used to meet Michelle secretly. That was the end of Dennis Watts. As Max Miller used to say of himself: 'There'll never be another.'

ANGIE WATTS

Albert Square's drama queen was Angie Watts, before she divorced Den and first went off to Spain, then later on the States, where she got married.

Angie's heart was always breaking and usually her husband Den was the cause, but her professionalism as a pub landlady and her tough 'Cockney sparrer' style kept her going, hiding the tears with a mask of make-up and a mile-wide smile.

Angie laughs a lot and appears to love everyone she meets. Her habitual gaiety isn't an act; it is a kind of affirmation of the life force. 'Things couldn't be worse, but I'm still here,' she seems to be saying.

The jammy lipstick and the tarty clothes are a badge of defiance, a demonstration that whatever the world throws at Angie Watts, it can't destroy her. She tried to kill herself once, but it didn't work and maybe she didn't want it to. It was all a desperate ploy to prise Den away from his mistress, Jan.

Angie married Den at eighteen because she loved him and because every other girl around fancied him. Den was the jackpot. Then she found out that the jackpot had been devalued. Den wasn't the lover she dreamed of – for years they didn't make love at all – and he was a bastard to live with.

They adopted Sharon to bring themselves closer together, but Sharon caused even more rifts between them as she grew up.

Angie tried to keep up the fiction of a happy marriage in the Saloon Bar of The Vic, though Den didn't help by frequently slagging her off in public. She got her own back by flirting with every man she fancied and some she didn't. Often she went beyond just flirting. For a time she drank far too much, damaging The Vic's profits and her body at the same time.

For all Den's philanderings and her own wayward ways, Angie never stopped loving him. She never stopped trying to get him away from other women. Finally, to break the relationship with Jan, she lied to Den and told him she had only six months to live. He believed her and ended the affair, then handed her divorce papers on Christmas Day when he knew the truth.

Even after they were divorced Angie wanted him back. Kidney failure took her into hospital and Den paid a few uncomfortable visits. Sentimentally, she suggested they remarry and move away from the East End. Typically Den told her that he wouldn't marry her if she were the last bint in Walford.

So Angie went off to Spain with a lover, then later went to America and remarried. She keeps in touch with Albert Square through Sharon and maybe she'll return for a visit some day. She'll still be smiling and she'll still be suffering, that's for sure.

ANITA DOBSON

For a time, Anita Dobson was one of the best-known women in Britain while Angie and Dennis Watts were battling it out in Albert Square. She was in the show from the first episode until Angie finally left for sunny Spain in the spring of 1988.

Anita loved the fame. For thirteen years she had been beavering away as an actress, doing good work without receiving a lot of recognition. Then stardom! She made a record, 'Anyone Can Fall In Love', based on the show's theme tune, and it reached number one. She was voted Rear Of The Year, appeared on chat shows, in pantomime and in the papers.

Since leaving, Anita has done more good work, though her musical Budgie, *with Adam Faith, died a swift death. She had fine notices for the revived Tom Stoppard musical* Rough Crossing *and even better ones for her Holocaust survivor in* My Lovely . . . Shayna Maidel. *She also made a comedy for ITV called* Split Ends.

Anita, forty-two, is a real EastEnder who was born just off the Mile End Road, although she now shares grander accommodation in Holland Park with her rock star boyfriend, Brian May. If she lives to be a hundred and ends up as Director of the Royal Shakespeare Company, they'll still write on her tombstone: She was Angie Watts.

CINDY BEALE

 Pretty and blonde, Cindy is a nice convent girl to whom a lot of nasty things happened. Some people would say that most of them were her own fault, but then folks have been criticising this sweet-faced Cindy doll since she was a teenager.

She turned up in Walford working on her mother's hat stall in the market, and her reputation as a girl who slept around soon began to grow. But she was really just a healthy normal young woman with a healthy, normal interest in sex.

Cindy fell heavily in love with Simon Wicks (Wicksy) when he was working as a barman at The Queen Victoria, but at that time he was only interested in her as one of many casual girlfriends.

She started up a relationship with Ian Beale, who was two years younger than her, as a way of making Wicksy jealous. It didn't work, though she got pregnant by Wicksy after a one-night stand upstairs at The Vic.

So Cindy married Ian, who thought the baby was his. After Steven was born the pair moved in with Ian's father, Pete, in his tower block flat, but that didn't work out too well and eventually the couple moved into Colin Russell's old flat at 3 Albert Square. Cindy tried hard to make the marriage work and did what she could to help Ian in his growing catering business.

By this time Wicksy had a permanent relationship with Sharon Watts and they were talking of getting married. But Wicksy began to fret about baby Steven; Wicksy couldn't bear seeing Ian as a proud dad when he knew that he was the real father. He began to see Cindy and Steven secretly until Cindy and Wicksy were viewing themselves as a couple with a baby son.

Finally Cindy told Ian that he wasn't Steven's father and sent him screaming away in his van and into a near-fatal crash. Eventually she forced him to accept the truth.

Wicksy left Sharon for good and moved into the B & B with Cindy and baby Steven. They were a happy family but the pressures from the Beales – Pete kept telling them in his best John Wayne manner to 'git out of Walford' – finally forced them to leave the district.

Cindy, who started out as a naturally happy, open, friendly, cheeky, amusing girl, left the Square careworn, almost

MICHELLE COLLINS

At one time, Michelle Collins was a backing singer for Marie (The Beehive) Wilson, and she worked in many areas of show business before joining EastEnders. *As Cindy Beale, married to one man but loving another, she had to prove herself a serious actress, and that's exactly what she did.*

At first, the popular press regarded the blonde, sexy-looking girl as just a bit of glamour, but as Cindy's tragic storyline with Ian and Wicksy developed, they began to take her seriously. That suited Michelle. 'I've always been very serious about my career,' she says. 'I never wanted to be anything but an actress.'

Michelle left EastEnders *because the heavy schedules made it difficult for her to spend enough time with the man she loves, Nick Fordyce, who lived in Spain. After she left, she presented Channel 4's trendy late-night show* The Word, *recorded several songs and moved into films.*

110

downtrodden. With luck, a new life in another neighbourhood will bring her back to her old perky self.

SIMON WICKS

 Simon, or Wicksy as he was known, was well-liked in Albert Square until the trouble with Ian Beale and his wife Cindy. Then most of the locals sided with Pete and Ian in their determination to force Wicksy to leave the neighbourhood.

The ironic part is that for most of his life Simon thought that Pete was his father – and so did Pete. Just as Ian Beale thought he was baby Steven's father. (In Albert Square it's a very knowledgeable child that knows its own father.)

When Wicksy left with Cindy the Square lost its only sexy young man. There is a cheekiness about Simon Wicks that's very attractive. In his early days he was happy-go-lucky, interested only in girls and paying off his debts. Generous Pete managed the debts for him, but handsome Wicksy managed the

girls all on his own.

Sharon fancied him, so much so that she secretly went off for a weekend with him, but she came back a virgin 'because it didn't feel right'. But later on it did feel right with Wicksy and, later still, the pair started living together. Other girls in his life included Mags, the Polish girl from Yorkshire, who entered Simon's bed after she left Den's and got him the sack from The Vic, and, of course, Cindy Beale. In between, Simon put it about a bit, as they say in Albert Square. He probably inherited the habit from his mother, Big Pat.

It's surprising that anyone as bright as Simon never progressed beyond being a bartender. He did that at The Vic and The Dagmar and though he came back to The Vic as manager for a time it didn't last.

Maybe with the responsibility of Cindy and Steven to look after, the lad will capitalise on his real talents and get somewhere. He could probably make it as a musician. His bar-room piano was well-liked in The Vic and he can sing a bit. Perhaps he'll return to the Square one day as a visiting celebrity.

NICK BERRY

Being voted Britain's sexiest man gave Nick Berry, who played Simon Wicks (Wicksy), a good laugh, because he's really shy and prefers football to flirting. He had a number one chart hit with the song 'Every Loser Wins' in 1986, which gave him another laugh. 'My singing's awful', he said.

Nick had a horrific car crash when he was twenty-one: he fractured his skull when he was thrown through a windscreen. Miraculously, he survived the experience unscarred to become

the EastEnders' top pin-up, receiving the most fan mail so far.

He started acting at the age of eight, did a fair bit of stage and television work before EastEnders and wants to make it in films now he's left. He should manage it: he can act without the technique showing.

Nick drives a Jag, lives in an Islington penthouse and, since he stopped seeing Gillian Taylforth (who plays Kathy Beale), has become engaged to the model, Rachel Roberts.

GEORGE HOLLOWAY

Short-sighted and sweet-natured, George (Lofty) Holloway was the holy fool of Albert Square. A wimp, almost a simpleton, he shone with such genuine goodness that it was almost unbearable when Michelle aborted his baby and caused him to leave Walford.

Michelle could hardly bear it herself. She had already jilted him at the altar, even if she did relent later and allow Lofty to marry her. With honesty she told him that this was because she needed someone to look after herself and baby Vicki. With a look of pure love, Lofty took on the job. He'd never had anyone to care for, you see, and caring was what he was good at.

At least when he left the Square it was to do something that suited him. He became the caretaker of a children's home, and surely he was happy taking care. And mixing with people of his own mental age.

Lofty is tall and gawky, peers hesitantly through John Lennon specs and, like Hamlet, he has great trouble in making up his mind. As barman in The Queen Victoria he had even more trouble distinguishing mild from bitter; he took his time in giving the customers change and usually got it wrong. It was amazing that anyone as brisk as Dennis Watts kept him on, but even Den had charitable urges sometimes. Willmott-Brown gave him a job too, carrying out the squire's traditional duty to the peasants.

Lofty had been in the army, but asthma released him, which is just as well because he must have come in for some terrible mockery. In Albert Square Lofty should have been a figure of fun, too, but Walford saw his essential goodness and respected it.

TOM WATT

He may have looked like a gangly teenager but Tom Watt was actually thirty years old when he touched Britain's heart as George (Lofty) Holloway.

Lofty was a lovable simpleton: Tom has a degree in drama and a string of other qualifications. (It runs in the family: his mother was the first woman Professor of Economic History at Cambridge.)

Tom supports Arsenal, lives just round the corner from their Highbury ground, likes old cars, swims forty lengths a day and buys some of his clothes at Oxfam, though he's been seen in designer suits too. He's shy, a vegetarian and cares deeply about the world and its problems. He felt just-literate Lofty had something to teach well-educated Tom in the way of openly expressing his emotions.

Tom is a committed Labour Party member, speaks for left-wing causes (Lefty Lofty?), plays football for charity and once had Anita Dobson (Angie Watts) for a girlfriend.

Since leaving EastEnders he has worked regularly on stage and television and formed his own theatre company.

TONY CARPENTER

Despite being the head of Albert Square's first black family, Tony Carpenter didn't get a lot of respect. A builder and handyman, he's amiable and easy-going, but he missed the warmth of Trinidad, his home, judging by the sheepskin jacket and beret he seemed always to wear indoors and out. Maybe he should have borrowed Pete Beale's stetson, because he was certainly bit of a cowboy worker. He rarely finished a job, but to be fair, he never seemed to be paid for one, either.

Separated from his shrewish wife, Hannah, Tony lived with his unruly teenage son, Kelvin, in 3 Albert Square, which he was (slowly) converting into flats; clumsily, he did his best. Angie popped round one evening for a drink and an affair. Poor Tony took it seriously, but as soon as Angie had succeeded in annoying Den over it, she cast Tony off.

At one stage Hannah returned with their daughter, Cassie, and, to please the children, he agreed to try living together as one big unhappy family again. By May 1987 he had given up the effort, so he packed his tool kit, zipped up his sheepskin jacket and returned to the West Indies.

KELVIN CARPENTER

Surprisingly enough, Kelvin has turned out well, but there were problems along the way. As a schoolboy he had trouble with girls – fighting them off, that is. Sharon, Michelle and most of the other females of Walford seemed keen on him, but they were never half as keen as he was on himself. A musician, he was an active member of the Square's rock group, The Banned (which probably should have been just that), from the start. Later his college friends, such as O level socialist Harry Reynolds, tolerated the Walford folk. Kelvin's time with Carmel Roberts improved him but she saw through his dreadlocks and gave him the push. He left Albert Square in 1987 for university where, knowing Kelvin, he probably put his lecturers straight on one or two things.

HANNAH CARPENTER

'Hard-hearted Hannah' is just about right when it comes to Tony's wife, and she's a nagger, to boot. Neville, her fancy man (after she left Tony), couldn't take it, so he beat her up and was violent to young Cassie, too. Hannah may have tried to make things work again when she moved back with Tony, but it didn't show. Walford was not grand enough for her. Luckily.

CASSIE CARPENTER

Tony and Hannah's daughter, Cassie, was a mischievous youngster, but forgivably so. Bright, like her brother, she tried pot-smoking, so her horrified mother sent her to a boarding school. But Cassie ran away and came home, only to have to leave when Hannah decided to move on to greener pastures.

PAUL MEDFORD

Now twenty-three, Paul Medford played Kelvin Carpenter for three years and became one of the most popular young actors in the show. Born in West London of Barbadian parents, Paul is heavily into music. He released a record while still with EastEnders *and starred in the West End musical,* Five Guys Named Moe, *after he left.*

KENNY BEALE

Kenny was banished to New Zealand by Lou, his tyrannical mother, to avoid 'trouble' over his relationship with Pat while she was married to his brother, Pete. He returned to Albert Square for a short visit early in 1988, partly because his marriage had broken up and partly because he'd heard that Pat Wicks was on the scene again. Rumours abounded that Kenny, and not Pete as had been assumed until then, was the father of Pete's son, Simon Wicks.

Poor Kenny didn't have much of a holiday while he was in Walford, what with lectures from Lou, fights with Pete and the news from Pat that he wasn't much cop as a lover. Later she added that Brian Wicks was Simon's father, actually. Kenny's daughter, Elizabeth, came with him, stayed longer and had a fling with Ian, although she got on Kathy's nerves by using the Beales' small flat as a hotel. When Pete won some money later that year, he spent it on a trip to New Zealand. It could be a long time before Kenny shows his face in Albert Square again.

COLIN RUSSELL

Colin and his young barrow boy lover, Barry Clark, were the only known gay men in Albert Square and it took the Square some time to get used to the idea. Eventually, though, Colin and Barry were seen as OK. They were tolerated, if not exactly welcomed, by older Walfordians. Pauline Fowler, who came in to clean for Colin, did an excellent public relations job for him, telling everyone what a nice bloke he was.

The phrase sums up Colin perfectly. He listens to everyone's troubles, then goes out of his way to help solve them in a smilingly unobtrusive fashion.

Colin's middle-class ways puzzled Walford. They were intrigued by his Filofax, uncertain about his tastefully restrained decor, unsure how to take his subtle humour. For he was the first of the yuppies to invade the Square, and to be gay and middle-class was a double handicap.

Colin, a freelance graphic designer, kept

MICHAEL CASHMAN

After playing gay Colin Russell, Michael Cashman left EastEnders *to play a 'rampant heterosexual' on an Agatha Christie tour, then received high praise for his work in the harrowing play,* Bent, *about homosexuals under Nazism, with his friend Sir Ian McKellan. He has also presented a BBC documentary about attitudes to gay people, written a novel,* Bloody Soap, *and staged an art sale which raised money for the campaigning gay rights charity, Stonewall, of which he's a director with, among others, Pam St Clement.*

Michael lives in the East End with actor Paul Cottingham and remembers Albert Square fondly.

'Quite a few gay activists thought Colin too nice but I thought he was just right. There was a fuss about his kiss with Barry which was sad – people should be upset by demonstrations of hate, not of love. And I was sorry the scene where Barry's father disowned him was cut out.'

going when Barry left him for a hetero lifestyle, and formed an uneasy relationship with another middle-class gay called Guido. But a strange illness – Colin thought it could be Aids though it turned out to be multiple sclerosis – finally persuaded him to leave Albert Square and go and live with his brother in Bristol. He hasn't been back to Walford since.

BARRY CLARK

Colin's boyfriend, Barry sold records in the market and hoped that his Dad wouldn't discover he was gay. 'He'd kill me if he found out,' he used to tell Colin, who found working-class prejudice against the people they called queers and poofters hard to understand.

Eventually Barry told his thug brother Graham and discovered that Graham had already guessed. Then Barry told his dad and came out of the experience alive. Not long afterwards, though, he developed an interest in girls, not because his sexuality was really changing but because the pressure to conform was just too much for him.

JAN HAMMOND

It was a chalk and cheese love affair but Jan Hammond was Dennis Watts' mistress for seven years. The relationship worked as long as elegant, sophisticated P.R. girl Jan stayed outside Den's working-class world at The Vic.

When Angie and Sharon left the pub Miss Silk Knickers (Angie's name for Jan) moved in. It was a mistake. She couldn't stomach living in a grotty room over a tatty pub and she found it difficult to be gracious to Den's rougher regulars.

The couple broke up and Jan went off with an old Italian flame, Dario. Den was heart-broken but managed to keep going until he met his next regular girlfriend, Polish caterer Mags.

NAIMA JEFFERY

Many of the problems which confront Asian women in Britain today have been faced by Naima. Born here of Bangladeshi parents, she is a Moslem but Westernised. She learned to cope with her nickname of 'Paki' at school, but Naima never fitted into life in Albert Square. But then she never chose to. Her parents forced her into marriage with Saeed, her cousin, and pushed the pair into running the Bridge Street grocery store when they had to make a sudden return to Bangladesh. Yet the marriage was doomed. Naima refused to sleep with Saeed at first, and then discovered to her horror that he was responsible for the dirty phone calls going round the Square, had been to the strip club where Mary worked, and had slept with a prostitute.

It took courage to walk out but that's what Naima did. She moved in with Debs and tried to run the corner shop when her sad and mixed-up husband went back to Bangladesh. She cut her hair and even tried to flirt with Wicksy. More importantly, she transformed the shop into a modern mini-market and made a success of it, despite racist daubings and threats from local villains. Then her cousin Rezaul from

Birmingham turned up to muscle in on the action, and graciously announced he would marry her; she told him where to stick his charity. Naima was hostile to Farrukh, the next cousin sent by the family as a marriage prospect, but happily she found she fancied him and a few months later left for Bangladesh to be his bride. Maybe marriage will be happier for her second time around.

ASHRAF KARIM

Ashraf was never *that* happy in Albert Square, but it wasn't the Square's fault. He'd come to Britain in 1968 and was already engaged to Sufia, who was still a child in Bangladesh. Before he returned home to be married, he met and had a fling with Stella, a young hippy, and their relationship continued on and off after Sufia emigrated to Britain to be with her husband in 1973. Serious and often stern-faced, Ashraf enjoyed women's company and saw nothing wrong in having casual affairs; he squared them with his Moslem faith. Sufia, who was more 'Western', knew about Stella, suspected some of the other affairs and found them all distressing.

At the beginning, Ashraf worked in a car manufacturing plant in the Midlands. Later on, relatives in Walford offered him a job in one of their corner shops and he, Sufia and their two small children came south. He soon saved enough money to open a business of his own, although racist taunts and attacks made life difficult. Even so, by putting in long hours he finally made a success of running his third shop in Walford High Street. In 1988 he employed cousins there, leaving him free to buy and run the First Till Last shop in Bridge Street owned by Naima, originally with Saeed, Ashraf's second cousin. The family moved into the house Julie Cooper owned in Victoria Road, and Shireen and Sohail, both bright, attended a private school.

The Karims kept themselves to themselves but when their teenage children mixed with Ricky and Diane Butcher, and Shireen babysat for Michelle, there was some breaking of the cultural ice. Arthur worked in the shop for a while, though typically it wasn't a success.

Sneaky Sohail was keen on Diane and leaned on Ricky to try to fix up a date for him, threatening to tell about Ricky's innocent hours alone with Shireen when she was minding Vicki. Pretty Shireen liked Ricky as a friend but her father, outraged by her forwardness, marched her off to Dr Legg for a virginity test which the wise physician refused to perform.

When Ashraf decided to solve the Shireen-and-boys 'problem' by arranging a marriage for her, the plan rebounded on him. To Shireen's delight, the chosen partner, Jabbar, was charming and enlightened and the pair became genuinely attached. Some time later, though, Jabbar's uncle spotted Ashraf with Stella in a restaurant and realised the Karim family were not as they'd seemed. The uncle cancelled the engagement and Shireen was left mystified and upset, while Sufia felt angry and betrayed. The solution Ashraf chose was to leave the shop in the hands of the cousins and move the family to Bristol.

Happily, before they left, Sufia and the women of Jabbar's family helped the young couple to meet secretly. They continue to write. Perhaps the engagement's back on by now.

JULIE COOPER

 She's a tough nut, is Julie, although life has delivered its fair share of cracks. She was born in Walford, then moved to Salford with her mum (who was a prostitute) as a small girl. In June 1989 Julie came back to live in the house left to her by her grandma Sylvia (who was also no better

than she ought to be, according to Lou Beale). A hairdresser and beautician, who is proud of her own mane of blonde curls and sexy looks, Julie likes a good time too, but she's nobody's plaything.

She'd lived with Billy, but he two-timed her and no one, she vowed, would hurt her again. A further sadness knowing she could never have children. So Julie decided she would be her own boss, and invested her savings in having the chip shop converted into Julie's Salon.

Seducing young builder Paul Priestley was a bit of fun. Too bad if Diane Butcher was jealous! And what did it matter if Kathy, her pal, was keen on Laurie Bates for a while? Julie used him in the meantime, along with Grant Mitchell. Julie added colour to Albert Square and Albert Square added wisdom to Julie. Its old ladies and young kids became her family. She proved she could make a new life for herself.

Michelle enjoyed working with Julie and so did young Marie Davis. The trouble for Julie was you don't get rich perming Ethel's wigs or giving Dot shampoos and sets. The business went bust and Julie went back north, a little older and wiser, but still the life and soul of the party.

LOUISE PLOWRIGHT

Residents of Chorley, Lancashire, may remember Louise Plowright, who played cocksure Julie Cooper, in her previous job as the manager of a shoe shop. She enjoyed amateur dramatics and at the ripe old age of twenty-seven got brave, applied and was accepted by Bristol Old Vic Drama School.

When she auditioned for EastEnders the casting director was dubious. Louise, then thirty-three, didn't look old or tough enough to play this serious man-eater. 'So I really played up the Bette Midler act,' said Louise. 'That did it.' But the actress, who has gone on to work on stage and as a private detective in the television drama series, Palmer, admits she never picked up Julie-style flirting. 'If a man stares romantically at me, I'm more inclined to grin, wave back and go "Coo-ee!"'.

PAUL PRIESTLEY

A nice-looking lad from Leeds, Paul came down to London with the building firm he worked for, then decided to go it alone. His first job was to convert Julie's shop into a hairdressing salon. The money wasn't great but there were benefits – for instance, Julie discussed his estimates in bed. Paul lodged at The Vic where Diane, sweet sixteen, thought he was wonderful (he agreed), and she even forgave him when she found out about Julie. Paul was a good pal to Trevor Short, who was more of a liability than a labourer. When work on the Karims' house came to an end, Paul decided to return home, where another smitten girl awaited him. Diane was heart-broken and ran away shortly afterwards. Decently, Paul popped back to assure her dad that he knew nothing of her whereabouts, then caught the train back to Leeds and, no doubt, a string of anxious admirers.

MARGE GREEN

Brown Owl of the 1st Walford Brownies, Marge was an innocent, a spinster who yearns for love and deserves it. She was always more of a mouse than an owl, a funny, easily flustered frump who was scared of men and the modern world because she'd hidden away from both for most of her life. In her youth, she was briefly engaged to a soldier but he married her best friend. She'd worked as a cleaner at the bed and breakfast guest house when it was run by

MARK THRIPPLETON

Just like his character, Paul Priestley, Mark Thrippleton comes from Leeds and has a Yorkshire accent you can cut with a knife. And, like Diane's builder boyfriend, he was a roofer and tiler before the acting bug bit. There the similarities end. Mark wishes he had Paul's nerve with girls. 'I'm a bit shy, me. I'd have schoolboy crushes and girls wouldn't want to know because I was small and thin for my age. I thought about being a jockey. To stop being picked on at school, I started to do impersonations, make people laugh.'

Weight-training and keep-fit got rid of his weedy look but the twenty-three-year-old jokes that he's still not a smooth operator with women and wonders if he should have played Paul's pal, daft Trevor, instead. 'I once drove my car on to the beach at Blackpool and the yacht club had to dig me out before the police came. It was dead embarrassing.'

PAT COOMBS

Already known and loved as one of Britain's best comedy actresses, Pat Coombs relished her role of Brown Owl Marge Green. She had joined her local Girls' Life Brigade as a ten-year-old growing up in south east London, but the young Pat was never able to wear the uniform because her parents couldn't afford it. Now in her early sixties, Pat was a radio 'playmate' of Arthur Askey, Irene Handl and gang and has partnered almost every top comedian, including Eric Barker, Reg Varney, Terry Scott, Ronnie Corbett and, of course, Dick Emery. Like Marge, she's a spinster. 'I really should have married,' she smiles.

Doris. Poor Marge was put upon by her domineering ninety-three-year-old mother, and the antics of young Melody and other 'bovver girl' Brownies were getting her down too. Friendless, except for Tibby, her mother's cat, Marge was pleased to let tough Mo Butcher muscle into the Brownie pack and then found friends in Dot, Ethel and Walford's odd-jobbers, Paul and Trevor. Briefly she helped at the launderette, but she would muddle up the service washes.

Everything changed when her mother died. Marge was on a short dancing holiday and had just met, conquered but rejected debonair Mr Conroy when the news came through. He'd left before she could tell him she was free after all. Now she's a paid companion travelling the world, and is sadly missed by many Walfordians. Maybe love will find her in foreign climes.

LAURIE BATES

Apparently carefree and as nice as they come, Laurie Bates upset Pete Beale twice when he arrived in Walford. First he took a pitch in the market to run a rival fruit and veg stall (his family have several in markets around London). Then he set his cap at Kathy Beale, asked her out and was understanding when she said she couldn't be rushed after her rape ordeal and there'd be none of 'that'. Even so, the knowledge of his other women, especially his late wife (she died of cancer) and his casual fling with Julie Cooper, annoyed Kathy. She realised that Laurie had hidden shallows; he wasn't the one to restore her faith in men. So he left Walford, bruised like a dropped apple.

TREVOR SHORT

He shambled into Albert Square in the summer of 1989, looking for something. What was it now? Oh, yes, his pal, Paul Priestley. Trevor isn't bright; 'two biscuits short of a box' they used to say in The Vic. The Karims, whose house he tried to help decorate, probably wouldn't give him a job reference.

Life hasn't been a picnic for this teenager, though. He was in and out of children's homes as a kid and never felt he belonged. He's quite harmless, as Diane and Shireen, over whom he mooned, would confirm. Mo Butcher took him in as a lodger and enjoyed bossing him around, but then he left. Somewhere, Trevor's smiling, bodging a job, and trying to make some friends.

PHIL McDERMOTT

Phil McDermott heard the EastEnders *team were looking for a tall Scot to play Trevor, the dim-witted odd job man who drifted into Albert Square. As he's short, comes from an Irish family and is brightly articulate, the twenty-seven-year-old Londoner knew some serious acting was required. He landed the job by crying for five minutes on cue and grew to like Trev.*

He also had sympathy for a young man who had drifted: Phil was a trainee priest who forswore the cloth, then took up scrap metal work, weighbridge operating and carpentry before going to drama school. 'My reason for becoming an actor was that I couldn't hold down a steady job and I wanted to have a laugh,' he admits.

CARMEL ROBERTS JACKSON

If anyone deserved a medal for patience it was Carmel Roberts when she was working as Albert Square's health visitor. West Indian by origin, British by education and saintly by nature, Carmel was landed with all the long-term losers, Mary Smith, Sue Osman, Donna Ludlow and Arthur Fowler among them. When she moved into the ground floor flat at 3 Albert Square, her racketeer brother, Darren, dumped his children, little Aisha and delinquent Junior, on her. Her handsome hunk of a husband, Matthew Jackson, turned out to be an emotional mess with a violently jealous streak. He beat her savagely once, then flew at her after she took a working lunch with Dr David. Junior, defending Carmel, accidently wounded Matthew with a knife. Her sister, Maxine, seemed a selfish piece and long-suffering Carmel eventually had to leave the Square in 1989 to help someone else – her newly widowed mother.

MAGDA CZAJKOWSKI

Known as Mags because her real name is such a mouthful, Magda Czajkowski is half-Polish, half-Yorkshire, so she can polish off a Yorkshire pudding in no time. Not that Mags ever cooked anything as ordinary as that. She came into the Square as an upmarket caterer and Dennis Watts soon got a taste for her goodies.

She couldn't stand Den's masterful ways for long and switched her affections to the more manageable Wicksy. But getting Mags into the sack earned Wicksy the sack from The Vic, when Den found out what was happening.

Clever, energetic and hardworking, Mags is still around somewhere in the catering business, giving Ian Beale competition in the posh nosh game.

HAZEL

A sharp little piece, Hazel is a former girlfriend of Nick Cotton. She conned Dot Cotton into believing that Nick was the father of her baby Dorothy Nicola (named after Dot and Nick). Dot was overjoyed at being given a grandchild and helped Hazel out with money, but finally discovered the girl was lying.

The baby belonged not to Hazel but to her sister, and the child's name was really Katy Joanna. Hazel apologised, soft-hearted Dot forgave her and Hazel met and fancied Rod the punk.

Nick beat her up and put her in hospital, but Rod visited and he and Hazel became a couple. Maybe he has helped her to mend her ways.

ROD NORMAN

Punk and philosopher, Rod Norman is nicer than he looks. His dreadful black greasy hair and clothes that could do with a couple of days' non-stop swishing in Dot's launderette, cover a kind heart, a compassionate nature and a quirky way of looking at the world.

Rod arrived in the Square as Mary Smith's boyfriend but she threw him out when he failed to pick up little Annie from the nursery one day. Later he took over Barry's record stall, passing it on to Donna when he left to tour Europe with a girl punk rock group. When he got back Donna was addicted to heroin and Rod blamed himself for her plight.

For a time he lodged in Dot Cotton's flat with Hazel, but then it was time to move on. Moving day arrives at regular intervals for Rod; he'll never settle down.

JAMES WILLMOTT-BROWN

He may look and talk like a proper gent but James Willmott-Brown raped Kathy Beale and got three years inside for it.

An ex-Army officer and a super-smoothie, Willmott-Brown took over a rough pub called The Dagmar and refurbished it as a yuppy alternative to Dennis Watts' The Vic. The bar was tastefully furnished but it never really appealed to the residents of Walford. Willmott-Brown brought in Angie Watts as manager and when she moved on he invited Kathy Beale to run things.

He fancied her, but although she sometimes found her husband Pete a bit heavy-going, Kathy had no intention of being unfaithful to him. One night Willmott-Brown invited her to his quarters upstairs and, mistaking her friendliness for acquiescence, raped her.

He then ran off into the night. Later Den set light to The Dagmar, partly to rid himself of the competition, partly in line with an old East End tradition that says you deal with problems personally instead of calling in the law.

Willmott-Brown had been on bail for six months when he emerged from a dark night to try bribing Kathy to drop the case. She was terrified and ran. But later she co-operated in getting Willmott-Brown caught in a police trap as he tried to hand over the bribe money. He hired a sharp defence lawyer but in the end the truth of Kathy's story was accepted.

If you met James Willmott-Brown, you'd think he was a charming chap. Unless you knew what he did to Kathy Beale, that is.

ANDY O'BRIEN

Tall and good-looking, Andy O'Brien was a Scottish nurse who lived with pretty Debbie Wilkins until he was run over and killed, heroically shoving a small child out of the path of an oncoming lorry. Andy was a man with a heart; he gave up his free time to teach punk Mary Smith to read, although Mary mistook his interest in her for love. Andy was the nearest Albert Square ever got to a straightforward hero, and they remember him with affection.

DEBBIE WILKINS

Determined and ambitious, blonde Debbie gave up her steady job in the bank to start her own business in Walford with the aim of making money fast. But this led to dreadful rows with the man she lived with, Andy O'Brien, a nurse at the local hospital.

Debs is a bossy girl and not everyone in Albert Square took to her. When Andy was killed in a tragic road accident, saving the life of a small child, she worked for a time in Naima's shop. Then the long arm of the law wrapped itself comfortingly about her; she was courted by Det. Sgt Quick but married Det. Sgt Rich. So she did manage to get Rich Quick – but in reverse order – before leaving the Square.

SUE OSMAN

Some people seem to be dogged by tragedy and Sue Osman is one of them. Always mentally unstable, she finally flipped completely when her husband Ali snatched their baby, Little Ali, from her as she was mourning at the grave of their toddler Hassan, who died in a cot death incident.

It was too much and Sue finally lost her grasp on reality, never all that strong at the best of times. She was put into what Albert Square euphemistically calls a home.

Perhaps they will let her out one day to enjoy life again. Because although she was always a bit of a moaner, Sue did enjoy life a lot. She loved her Turkish Cypriot husband in spite of his disastrous gambling, loved her friends and loved her babies while she had them. But she certainly had her problems. There was a time when Sue thought she had breast cancer and another when she went through a phantom pregnancy, and she earned the sympathy of Albert Square on both occasions.

They often think about her in that home, though only old friend and Samaritan Kathy Beale ever goes to see her there.

SANDY RATCLIFF

A lot of hearts were touched by Sandy Ratcliff when she played tragic Sue Osman, but her own life has been full of problems, too. She got into trouble with the police over drugs, and admitted that she was a heroin addict at one time.

Sandy was always a bit of a rebel, getting expelled from school at twelve and smoking pot by the time she was fourteen. She worked as a waitress, disc jockey, model and guitarist in a rock group. She married at twenty but it didn't last. Lord Snowdon picked her as the Face of the Seventies and she moved into films, playing a schizophrenic in the critically acclaimed Family Life.

Television work followed: Minder, Shelley, Target, Shoestring – *and then* EastEnders. *She has a son of seventeen, whom she calls 'the most important consideration of my life.'*

Since leaving the show things have been professionally quiet for Sandy, who is now forty, though her private life has brought her into the headlines again.